D0499130

"Randy Clark has produced perhap[...] useful study on the 'hows' of healing. His vast ministry experience has generated an exceptionally thoughtful, practical and biblical analysis of faith and healing—an analysis scientifically verified to doctoral dissertation standards in many thousands of real-world healing contexts."

Jon Mark Ruthven, Ph.D., professor emeritus of theology, Regent University School of Divinity

"Randy Clark's latest book, *The Healing Breakthrough*, so perfectly accomplishes what it seeks to do: It helps us dissolve and remove the 'rubble' of broken theology and disappointments regarding healing as it builds and rebuilds our faith in the miraculous power of God to restore. Both instructive and inspiring, Randy's anecdotes and extensive research are skillfully paired to impart foundational knowledge about how to pray for healing and why healings occur, as well as to remind us to follow the leading of the Holy Spirit and to realize what God is doing in the moment and to bless it."

Dr. Ché Ahn, apostle, Harvest Apostolic Center, Pasadena, California; apostolic leader, HRock Church; president, Harvest International Ministry; international chancellor, Wagner Leadership Institute

"This amazing book is so real, fascinating, inspiring and readable. It helps in building our solid walls of faith for healing, removing the rubble, finding priceless resources for building faith and generating an atmosphere that ushers in a healing breakthrough. Dr. Clark sets up a far-reaching milestone for the coming generations of healing ministry."

Andrew S. Park, professor of theology and ethics, United Theological Seminary

"I have learned a great deal from Dr. Randy Clark over the years, both from his books and from personal conversations. Here he once again lays out practical, theologically sound advice for anyone who wants to know more about God's gift of healing. This book is a gift to the Church. Highly recommended!"

David F. Watson, Ph.D., academic dean, vice president of academic affairs, associate professor of New Testament, United Theological Seminary

THE
HEALING
BREAKTHROUGH

Other Books by Randy Clark

Anointed to Heal (with co-author Bill Johnson)
Authority to Heal (book and curriculum)
Baptized in the Spirit
The Biblical Guidebook to Deliverance
Changed in a Moment
Entertaining Angels
The Essential Guide to Healing (book and curriculum kit,
with co-author Bill Johnson)
The Essential Guide to the Power of the Holy Spirit
Finding Victory When Healing Doesn't Happen (with Craig Miller)
The Healing Breakthrough
Healing Energy: Whose Is It? (with Susan Thompson)
Healing Is in the Atonement: The Power of the Lord's Supper
The Healing River and Its Contributing Streams
Lighting Fires
Power, Holiness and Evangelism
Power to Heal (book and curriculum)
Supernatural Missions (compiler and contributor)
There Is More!

Ministry Materials
Ministry Team Training Manual
School of Healing and Impartation (SHI) Workbooks:
SHI Kingdom Foundations (Revival Phenomena and Healing)
SHI Healing: Spiritual and Medical Perspectives
SHI Empowered (Deliverance, Disbelief, and Deception)

THE
HEALING
BREAKTHROUGH

CREATING AN ATMOSPHERE
OF FAITH FOR HEALING

RANDY CLARK

Chosen

a division of Baker Publishing Group
Minneapolis, Minnesota

© 2016 by Randy Clark

Published by Chosen Books
11400 Hampshire Avenue South
Bloomington, Minnesota 55438
www.chosenbooks.com

Chosen Books is a division of
Baker Publishing Group, Grand Rapids, Michigan

Printed in the United States of America

ISBN 978-0-8007-9783-6

Library of Congress Control Number: 2016930709

Unless otherwise indicated, Scripture quotations are from the Holy Bible, New International Version®. NIV®. Copyright © 1973, 1978, 1984, 2011 by Biblica, Inc.™ Used by permission of Zondervan. All rights reserved worldwide. www.zondervan.com

Scripture identified NIV 1984 taken from the HOLY BIBLE, NEW INTERNATIONAL VERSION®. Copyright © 1973, 1978, 1984 Biblica. Used by permission of Zondervan. All rights reserved.

Scripture quotations identified NKJV are from the New King James Version®. Copyright © 1982 by Thomas Nelson, Inc. Used by permission. All rights reserved.

Scripture quotations identified NRSV are from the New Revised Standard Version of the Bible, copyright © 1989, by the Division of Christian Education of the National Council of the Churches of Christ in the United States of America. Used by permission. All rights reserved.

Scripture quotations identified KJV are from the King James Version of the Bible.

The names and certain identifying details of some individuals have been changed in order to protect their privacy.

Cover design by Gearbox

20 21 22 23 24 25 26   9 8 7 6 5 4 3

I dedicate *The Healing Breakthrough* to the memory of Dr. Charles Price, whose book *The Real Faith* I have read many times.

I also dedicate *The Healing Breakthrough* to John Wimber, Omar Cabrera and Blaine Cook, who first modeled for me the connection between understanding what God is doing in a meeting and faith for healing and miracles.

Finally, I dedicate *The Healing Breakthrough* to Bill Johnson, who is sensitive to moving from his faith to the faith of God. Bill models living in faith, by faith, always desiring to increase the measure of faith he has.

CONTENTS

Foreword by Bill Johnson   11

Acknowledgments   15

Introduction: How Healing Moved from Rare to
Regular   17

**Part I: Obstacles to Creating an Atmosphere of Faith for
Healing   29**

1. Paul's Thorn in the Flesh   31
2. An Overemphasis on Sovereignty   35
3. The Big Lie about Faith   41
4. Harmful Hype   47
5. The Opposite of Hype   51
6. Expecting Too Much or Not Enough?   57
7. The Deception of Cessationism   59
8. A Deistic or Liberal Worldview   63
9. "Sickness Is My Cross to Bear"   67
10. Mistaking Emotionalism for Faith   70

11. Overreaction to the "Word of Faith" Position   76
12. Leaving the Rubble Behind   85

Part II: Building a Wall of Faith for a Healing Breakthrough   91

13. Back to Seminary at 59   93
14. Relating Spoken Words to Faith   101
15. Receiving Revelation   117
16. Faith and the Ways of God   125
17. Different Types of Faith   143
18. The Probability of Healing   155
19. Practical Applications   165
20. Contending for Breakthrough   174
21. Handling Unanswered Prayer for Healing   181
22. A Solid Wall of Faith for Healing   200

Notes   207
Index   215

FOREWORD

Randy Clark has been a close personal friend for almost twenty years. I met him in my quest for more of God. The stories of his impact in Toronto and elsewhere around the world had put a cry in my heart that could not be quenched with theory or ritual. All I hungered for was God Himself. I wanted Him to do something in my life that would change me from the inside out. I knew that the fruit of such a touch would be for me to have a greater impact on the world around me, which seemed like a wonderful benefit. It became obvious to me that Randy was a "carrier" of that kind of grace.

We met. And quite to my surprise, God gave me favor in his eyes. He came to Bethel Church here in Redding, California, and the rest is history. His deposit was not just for me; it was for our church family. Some things are too great to be given to an individual. They must be imparted to the Body as a whole.

Since Randy's first visit, healings and miracles have become a normal part of our life as a church. Interestingly, most of the miracles take place in public, where the people are. I cannot help but think that this is what Jesus modeled with His ministry in the marketplace and what He implied when He said for His disciples to "go into all the world." In other words, go where the people are. What many may not know, however, is that Randy is the primary figure in igniting and fueling that passion and gifting for healing that happens through Bethel's ministry.

One of my greatest joys in life is to join with Randy in traveling the earth in ministry, doing various conferences and healing schools and ministering in local churches. We are together around six to ten times a year, each event lasting for days, with many services a day. I say this only to emphasize that I have heard Randy teach and model the concepts in this book for years, and they never get old. They are absolutely priceless! I know of no one alive, or even anyone in Church history, who ministered healing with as clear an understanding of the subject.

But let me be clear. I am not talking about theory. The goal is not to have a great classroom discussion on healing. I am talking about the kinds of truths that release multitudes into their miracles while equipping them to bring healing to others.

The Healing Breakthrough might be the most important book I have ever seen on the subject of healing. This is quite a statement when you realize how many excellent books there are with both insights and stories of miracles filling their pages. Yet I make this statement for three reasons.

First, in my opinion, Randy really is an apologist. He has a grasp of Scripture that is rare. Even his stories are filled with revelation of Scripture. His vast knowledge of Church history enables him to see where healing movements in the past have failed and what parts of Scripture were neglected. He is also able to dissect the objections people have to the healing ministry with grace, yet with the biblical boldness needed to follow the example Jesus gave us when He said, "Greater works than these shall you do."

The second reason I say this is that Randy has no desire for recognition, fame or glory. I see this reality in and out of the pulpit. His passion is to be faithful to his call and to bring glory to the name of Jesus. This is most pronounced in his insistence on equipping the people of God to do the work of the ministry. He refuses to do things that would cause a congregation to become dependent on him. His transparency in the process of a healing meeting is both disarming and educational. He makes everyone realize that they can do it, too. That is an outcome that is rare indeed.

The final reason is that what Randy teaches in this book will save those wanting to see God use them in healing from years and years of heartache. I honestly don't remember any book or teaching series that addresses the questions Randy does so thoroughly in *The Healing Breakthrough*. There are still many believers who have objections to praying for the sick, although their numbers are decreasing. Those objections are addressed right here in these pages.

The healing ministry is a ministry of the cross. It has great highs and deep lows. There are wonderful victories and very challenging disappointments. The healing ministry is not an easy road to take. But because of the journey Randy has been taking for decades, we can glean from his insights and experiences and be that much better equipped for the days ahead, bringing to Jesus the glory that He alone deserves.

Beliefs have behaviors attached to them. And I cannot imagine anyone who believes the life-giving truths contained in this book will not experience the *breakthrough* mentioned in the title. These insights will help readers step into their destiny of ministering to the sick with increasing faith, understanding and authority.

You now hold in your hand a treasure, worth its weight in gold. Literally. Please read it, live it and keep it on your shelf as a reference guide for the years to come. And by all means, let us give ourselves to see the name of Jesus lifted high in the earth because we did what He commanded us to do: "Heal the sick, raise the dead, cleanse the lepers, cast out demons. Freely you received, freely give" (Matthew 10:8 NASB).

Bill Johnson, senior leader,
Bethel Church, Redding, California;
author, *When Heaven Invades Earth*
and *The Power That Changes the World*

ACKNOWLEDGMENTS

I want to thank Trish Konieczny for being such a great editor and a pure joy to work with.

I also thank Jane Campbell for believing I had something to say that needed to be said, and for encouraging me to say it.

I thank my wife, DeAnne, for allowing me to write during the too-small amount of time that I am home. DeAnne loves God and His Kingdom, always putting them first during our forty years together.

Finally, I thank my personal assistant, Vicki Hennedy, for her valuable help in keeping me focused, and for her efforts to keep me on target in meeting my deadlines.

INTRODUCTION

How Healing Moved from Rare to Regular

In the heat of a crowded room, the sound of prayer was rising. Several teenagers sixteen years old and up were present, along with one twenty-three-year-old who, just a few weeks earlier, had been the most infamous drug pusher in the community. Several of these young new believers had been buying their drugs from this pusher, who is now pushing the Gospel for Jesus. Only a few weeks old in their faith at the time, all of those present in the room were engaged in a great fight for healing. These young ones were involved in the great Jesus movement. They were part of the several million young people who came to Christ in the late 1960s and early '70s, in the revival that seemed to start among the hippies and then spread out to other young people in North America and Europe.

These new believers had been delivered themselves from alcoholism and drug addictions, and a few of them had been healed. What was the great cause for which they were now crying out with such intensity? What united them in such abandoned expectation, such full and passionate prayer? They had been praying for almost half an hour for one person, a middle-aged man named Johnny Metcalf, who had severe cerebral palsy.

I was present in that prayer meeting, and Johnny was in our midst. We knew all things were possible as we prayed for his healing. We had not been taught unbelief, since most of us had been unchurched until a few weeks earlier. And I had known Johnny since I was a little boy. I used to be afraid of him. Johnny walked with great difficulty, swinging from side to side just to keep his balance as he tried to work his partially paralyzed legs. He could not speak a word. At best, his attempts at communication sounded like unutterable groans.

Johnny tried to go to church several times a week. He would hitchhike to the small country church I had attended as a boy, but he had a ride every Sunday to his home church, which I joined when I was sixteen. I had seen Johnny come into the services in the wintertime with snow-covered pant legs from where he had fallen. Yet, in spite of such terrible handicaps from birth, Johnny loved God. He knew that one day he would be handicapped no longer. He knew Jesus had died for him and had forgiven his sins, and he knew Jesus could deal with his sicknesses and birth defects. Yet Johnny primarily put his hope for healing into the next life.

The revival had caused our faith to rise, however, and to believe that all things were possible. We not only believed it; we expected it. So for about thirty minutes we had been beseeching heaven in that meeting, crying out for Johnny's miracle. It did not happen.

Were we disappointed? Yes! Johnny left this world the way he entered it—severely handicapped from cerebral palsy. But right now Johnny is no longer handicapped. He has entered into the joy that truly was set before him in the Gospel. He is free to speak clearly, free to run and jump, free never to be sick or grow old or weak again, for all eternity.

At this point in my Christian life, I have some understanding about why Johnny Metcalf was usually the first person during midweek services to stand and give his testimony of praise to God. Though no one could understand a word he tried to say, those few unintelligible syllables spoke volumes to those of us who witnessed Johnny's faith and dedication to his Savior. It would be another quarter of a century before I began to see people with strokes healed. (Strokes are similar in nature to the cause of cerebral palsy, brain injury often resulting from a lack of oxygen to the brain.) And though it has been a total of 45 years since that night when we prayed for Johnny, I still have not seen someone be healed of cerebral palsy. But I still pray. I still am encouraged.

Why am I encouraged? Because it took 35 years and many prayers for stroke victims before I witnessed a breakthrough. When it happened, it happened suddenly. In one 24-hour period I witnessed three healings of people paralyzed by strokes. One man and woman were healed in the same service. We had a preservice prayer time for the terminally ill, the paralyzed, those who could not walk without aid, and the blind and deaf. During this hour of preservice prayer and the hour of worship that followed it, my team and I prayed for many people.

Along with a few others, I split my time between the two stroke victims. The man was not a Christian. His wife had told me in the morning service that her husband was coming to church for the first time in his life that night. He had not been a good husband; he had been unfaithful, violent and an alcoholic. The woman was a Roman Catholic. In Brazil, great prejudice exists between Catholics and evangelicals (the Brazilian equivalent of our Protestants). It took much courage for this Catholic woman to come to a Pentecostal Evangelical church.

She came with her family and wore a veil over her head, clearly marking her out as the Catholic in our midst.

Both these people had similar problems resulting from their strokes. Both had a claw hand on the partially paralyzed left side of their body. The woman's stroke had also taken away her ability to speak. She could not make her mouth say what her brain was thinking.

For about two hours our team had been praying. I had to leave them so I could prepare to step into the pulpit to preach and minister. As my intern was putting the mic around my ear and positioning it, I looked out over the crowd and was shocked at what I saw. The unsaved man paralyzed from his stroke was clapping his hands. His claw hand was now normal, and he was singing praise to his newly found Savior, Jesus Christ. The Catholic woman was also clapping normal hands together. The claw of paralysis was gone from her body as well, and she was singing. Her speech had been restored. After 35 years of never seeing one stroke victim healed, I saw two healed in a single service.

The next day at another church in Rio de Janeiro, we saw a man who had been paralyzed for many years get out of his wheelchair and walk after prayer for healing. He, too, had been a stroke victim. After so many years going by with not one stroke victim healed, in 24 hours three had been healed. What was different?

I believe one of the differences was that we were hearing stories of God raising the dead in Mozambique from our friends Rolland and Heidi Baker. I had the privilege of interviewing the first two Mozambican pastors who had raised the dead, Johnny and Rego. This was at a time when there had not been hundreds raised from the dead, as there have been now, but only a handful. I knew that if God raised the dead after they had been deceased for over an hour, He had to rebuild not only all of their brain cells, but all of the cells in their bodies. Understanding the implications of this miracle changed what I truly believed was not only possible, but what was probable. Even more than probable—it actually was happening in Mozambique.

I wish I could say that the healing of stroke victims continued to happen on a regular basis, but that has not been my experience. Miracles still are not normative, although they occur more regularly than they once did. Healing, on the other hand, has become a normative experience. By way of definition, healings can happen naturally, although God can speed them up to happen much more quickly than normal, or they can happen supernaturally and be directly related to God's power. Miracles are more than healings and more than a quickening of the healing process. They cause something missing to appear, as in a creative miracle, or they cause something that is there but should not be there to disappear, as in a tumor disappearing. Both healings and miracles can be supernatural, regardless of how they happen.

For me, healing has become normative—an imperative from the very emphasis of Scripture itself. On a personal level, I saw this standard grow incrementally over time. It has not always been this way. What happened to change healing from being rare to regular? A couple things happened at a couple different times. In March 1984 I saw more healings than I had seen in my lifetime. This was when a Vineyard church team led by Blaine Cook came to my Baptist church. After the Vineyard team's visit, my church and I began to see healings on a regular basis. Every month we would see people get healed. Considering that prior to this visit I could count on both hands all the healings I had seen in my life, it was a major improvement.

The Vineyard team taught my church and me how to recognize words of knowledge, which resulted in some dramatic changes for us. Another teaching that brought us dramatic change was how to pray for those with physical needs. We learned to use a relational prayer model for healing that included five specific steps. In addition to what we learned, the activation of words of knowledge and the impartation for healing were extremely important in our resultant breakthrough.

The combination of these three foundational things—recognizing words of knowledge, using the Five-Step Prayer Model[1] and receiving an activation/impartation—was so important that over thirty years later, I continue teaching them through Global Awakening's schools and conferences.[2] It is vital that we learn the ways of God, especially when it comes to the causal relationship between words of knowledge, faith and gifts of healing and/or miracles. This causal relationship becomes evident to those who learn to recognize words of knowledge, who have learned to cooperate with God through the relational Five-Step Prayer Model, and who have received activation or impartation in ministry times. These things are all tied together.

Though the initial experience in 1984 shaped much of what characterizes my ministry of healing and impartation, an even greater breakthrough came a decade later. Beginning in January 1994, healing started to become somewhat normative. This was the occasion of the Holy Spirit's outpouring in Toronto, when I visited there to do a four-day meeting that turned into the longest protracted meeting in North American history—six nights a week for twelve and a half years. On the first night we saw a woman healed of a terminal condition. Many more healings also began to occur. Healing was becoming a reality every week, or so it seemed.

Then, after January 1995 healing became fully normative. It became a reality at almost every meeting where we prayed for the sick. Not only did it become normative; over time the kinds of healings became greater. In 2009 the healing of people with chronic pain or limited range of motion due to surgically implanted material began.

It is my assumption that healing should be standard for the Church, even though sometimes it is not. We need to address the most basic and fundamental question of why healings occur. That is my focus in these pages. Since 1984, I have been involved continuously in the ministry of praying for the sick, a practice that affords a relatively extensive breadth of experience. I have also spent over 28 years trying to gain a better understanding of the variables that can affect the probability of healings occurring, as well as what factors create an atmosphere for healing.

Healings occur at different times. Sometimes they occur when I am on the platform during a service. Other times they occur during my one-on-one ministry time off the platform. Healings also occur when my ministry team members pray on their own. I have seen healings follow words of knowledge, and I have also seen them occur spontaneously during worship. I have seen people healed when they try to do what they previously could not do. I have seen people healed through watching a video that shows other people being healed. Sometimes the people God heals and how He heals them surprises me.

These "surprise" healings I have seen are the first of three reasons that I believe the critics of healing are incorrect. In light of these surprise healings, the critics' naturalistic explanations and placebo explanations are simply untenable. (Those are based on the humanistic understanding that it is faith that heals, not divine power.) The second reason the critics are mistaken is that for certain types of healings or miracles, the internal body-mind-spirit mechanism clearly cannot be used as an explanation. This is true for the phenomenon of raising the dead, especially where the person has been dead for more than an hour. The third reason is the inconsistent prayer results when one person prays for different people. For example, someone might pray for ten different people and see nothing happen to six of them, while two receive complete healing and two receive partial healing. This causes us to recognize that healing is not dependent on the person who prays, but rather on the power or energy of God that works through him or her (although not necessarily on a consistent basis).

One of these surprise healings happened in a city in Colorado where I was conducting a meeting. A woman came who was not expecting a healing and did not even believe in healing through prayers in Jesus' name. In fact, she had come to the School of Healing and Impartation we were holding (now called *Kingdom Foundations*) to mock me and criticize my meetings and ministry. The sister of a local professional, she stood in the back as a critical observer. Right there in the back—despite her attitude—she suddenly was healed. The woman's brother, a believer, shared this story with me a few days after her healing occurred. From that point on, her criticism ceased. Critics who say that "the power of suggestion" could be an explanation for some healings cannot hold their ground in a case like this, where the woman who got healed was not even open to healing in the first place.

I have met several people who reported that they were raised from the dead, and I have interviewed their families to confirm the reports. I have also visited villages that were once Muslim, but are now predominantly Christian because the people in the village confirmed reports of the dead being raised. After interviewing the humble people whom God used to raise the dead, and after seeing the effects of such miracles on a nation like Mozambique, I can say without a doubt that a naturalistic explanation of faith as a placebo simply does not suffice to explain all the relevant evidence.[3] In Mozambique alone, ten thousand new churches have been started and one million people have accepted Jesus due to healings and miracles, especially the raising of the dead.[4]

Even for me, with my many years of experience, healings can be inconsistent. For example, two brothers came for prayer in a meeting in southern India. Neither of them was able to walk due to having the same condition in their legs. I prayed for both and one was healed, while the other showed no improvement. There may have been a difference in each brother's expectations, but no one can really know the inner workings of their minds regarding healing. In this case, however, I believe what was most important in the one brother's healing was my faith as the person ministering. Many times, it is not the faith of the person in need of healing that determines whether a healing occurs; it is the faith of the person who is ministering that often is determinative. Both these brothers were Hindus, so my faith as the one praying was the determinative factor. But it is interesting to note that my level of faith was the same for each brother at the start. In fact, it was higher for the second brother after I saw that the first one was healed. My expectation was that the second brother would also be healed, yet he was not—which demonstrates that God's power is beyond our human expectation or our faith level.

Another example of this inconsistency dates back to 1984. John Wimber had allowed me to shadow him at several healing meetings. My instructions were to watch and listen, and at the end of the meeting to ask John any questions I had about what I observed. One night at a Methodist church in Houston, almost every person John prayed for was healed. The following night no one he prayed for was healed.

At the end of the second night, I said, "John, I have a question."

"Let me tell you what your question is," John responded. "You want to know why everyone was healed last night and no one was healed tonight, don't you?"

"Yes!" I said.

"You don't get it, do you?" John said. "Last night when everyone I prayed for was healed, I didn't go to bed thinking I was some great healer, or that I was somebody. And tonight when

I go to bed, I'm not going to be thinking I'm a great failure. I didn't have any more faith last night than I did tonight, and I don't have any more sin in my life tonight than I did last night. Tomorrow I will get up and pray for the sick again. All I did both nights was to stick my fat hand out and say, 'Come, Holy Spirit; I bless what I see You doing.'"

This dialogue with John was a turning point for me. I realized that the answer to seeing a breakthrough in healing was not some secret I needed to learn. Neither was it based on the merit of the person praying. It was wrapped in mystery. Yet as John demonstrated night after night, it was also related to faithfulness and our willingness to persevere in ministering God's love to those in need of healing.

In the missiological context, non-Christians often have not heard the Gospel, know nothing about the Christian faith (other than that it is not their faith), have not previously seen anyone healed in Jesus' name and have no theology of healing. Why do more people get healed in this context than in what would seem like a more conducive atmosphere—a Christian church service in a denomination that believes in healing, where people have heard the testimonies of others whom they know personally being healed, and where their faith for healing has been building through solid biblical teachings on the subject?

I believe the answer is the overriding desire of God to advance the Kingdom of God through salvation, which includes healing. For example, the greatest number of conversions I have ever seen happened during a meeting in India. One hundred thousand persons were gathered at the meeting, mostly Hindus. Fifty thousand of these were healed in one night, and thirty thousand accepted Jesus. This example begs the question of sovereignty in relation to healing, but it also relates sovereignty to soteriology, or the study of salvation. Another way to sum that up more simply is that where there is the preaching to people who have not heard the Gospel, the power to heal is present in an even greater degree, especially if the minister's theology includes the expectation of great outpouring of the Spirit on all flesh in the latter days. In this way sovereignty (God's freedom to act) is related to soteriology (the study of salvation). Where the power of the Holy Spirit causes many healings, it also softens the hearts of those who witness this compassionate power of God. It is true that God's goodness brings us to repentance!

Though healing is wrapped in mystery, we are beginning to understand some things about it better as we seek to understand the "ways of God" better. As Moses prayed in Exodus 33:13, "If you are pleased with me, *teach me your ways so I may know you and continue to find favor with you*" (emphasis added). Discovering the ways of God is related to knowing Him better and is key to finding favor with Him. The ministry of healing is much more successful when we stop focusing on trying to get God to bless what *we* are doing, and instead, we realize what *He* is doing and bless it. This is based on revelation from God out of our intimacy with God, and it is rooted in the operation of His gifts, which are what I call "gracelets" of His divine energy.

I call the gifts gracelets because they are tangible expressions of God's grace to a person. Grace is active, not just dismissive; it is enablement, not just forgiveness undeserved. Grace is also a demonstration of God's power when it is undeserved. Some commentators also refer to the charismata as gracelets. These are tangible, visible expressions in a small way of God's great ocean of grace.

Perhaps God has determined to link healing to the Gospel, intentionally making healing a sign that confirms it. Or, more accurately and biblically, perhaps healing is part of the Gospel and is included in the good news that Jesus bore our sins, sicknesses and sorrows on the cross. More good news is that the energy of the Kingdom of God has broken into our time and space, and that the energy of heaven has begun to come to earth.[5]

It is important to realize, however, that even Jesus is seen connecting words to the release of this energy in some cases, and He tells us the importance of our speech in relationship to the release of God's power to work healings and miracles. I will talk more about that concept and many others pertinent to healing ministry in part II of the book. In part I just ahead, we will look at some teachings that hinder the ministry of healing—obstacles that I see as theological "rubble" we need to clear away so that we can build a solid wall of faith for healing. We will deal with removing the rubble first, and then we will begin looking at the things that build faith and create an atmosphere more conducive to a healing breakthrough.

PART I

Obstacles to Creating an Atmosphere of Faith for Healing

The reason the Son of God appeared was to destroy the devil's work.

1 John 3:8

Several years ago I was in Minneapolis–Saint Paul, speaking at the International Charismatic Lutheran Conference. During one of the sessions, I felt led to speak on the obstacles to faith and healing. I drew upon the passage from Nehemiah where the people first had to clear away the rubble from the fallen places before they could rebuild the wall around Jerusalem. Using this story as a typological picture of the many issues that make faith in healing hard for people to have, I delivered an extemporaneous message on the subject. Deciding to "clear the rubble," I dealt with these challenges one by one. That is what I want to do in this part of the book—clear away the challenges that get in the way of people having faith in healing.

In the chapters just ahead, I will discuss what I call the rubble arguments about healing. One of them is Paul's "thorn in the flesh." Another is the issue of the relationship between God's sovereignty and healing, as expressed in the different worldviews the Church has embraced throughout its history.

I also will challenge the viewpoint I often heard in seminary, that superior faith is not dependent on signs and wonders. I will address the issue of how hype undermines true faith, and I will deal with the teaching that healing is not normative.

Of course, the big boulder we need to remove amongst the rubble is the argument that the gifts of healing and working of miracles ended with the canonization of the Bible. This argument would imply logically that there is no one today whom we could refer to as a healer or worker of miracles.

In addition, I will discuss a viewpoint that is actually stronger in Catholicism than in Protestantism, although many Protestants still believe it—the idea that "this sickness in my body is my cross to bear."

A further piece of rubble I find that often has to be removed all around the world is the way people confuse emotionalism with faith or praying through. And finally, I will deal with liberalism. This worldview does not believe that anything supernatural really occurred in the Bible or in history. It is based on an understanding of reality that cannot accept the supernatural, and it had its origins in eighteenth- and nineteenth-century scientific views that saw the world as a machine that ran on the laws of nature. Its proponents were convinced that those laws could not be broken without doing violence to reality.

These are the pieces of theological rubble that stand in the way of so many people receiving healing. Let's clear them away one by one, and then go on to build a wall of faith for healing.

1

Paul's Thorn in the Flesh

Remember the *wonderful works* He has done, His
miracles.

1 Chronicles 16:12 NRSV, emphasis added

I have been in the ministry for forty-five years. I spent thirty of
those years pastoring a total of seven local churches, three of
which my wife, DeAnne, and I planted. During all these years,
I have come across few beliefs that are as damaging to the
ministry of healing as the belief that sickness is a thorn in the
flesh that God sends to make us more holy or keep us humble.

Throughout my years of ministry, I have sat by the hospital
beds of many people who could not believe for healing because
they misunderstood Paul's thorn in the flesh. Instead of fighting the good fight of faith, these people accepted their sickness
as coming from God. How can someone pray in faith, asking
God to take away an illness He has sent? This is the faulty logic
behind the teaching that Paul's thorn in the flesh was an illness
sent by God.

When I wanted to pray for a person's healing in some of the churches I pastored in my younger days, I would be told, "No, Pastor, just pray that I'll be strong in this time of sickness, and that I'll know God's grace is sufficient." On other occasions I would be told, "Pastor, remember that even Paul wasn't healed when he asked for it; he was told God's grace would be sufficient."

From the time I was a small child, I can remember people using 2 Corinthians 12:1–10 as the answer to why God did not heal them. Let's look at this passage and its connection to healing.

> I must go on boasting. Although there is nothing to be gained, I will go on to visions and revelations from the Lord. I know a man in Christ who fourteen years ago was caught up to the third heaven. Whether it was in the body or out of the body I do not know—God knows. And I know that this man—whether in the body or apart from the body I do not know, but God knows—was caught up to paradise. He heard inexpressible things, things that man is not permitted to tell. I will boast about a man like that, but I will not boast about myself, except about my weaknesses. Even if I should choose to boast, I would not be a fool, because I would be speaking the truth. But I refrain, so no one will think more of me than is warranted by what I do or say. To keep me from becoming conceited because of these surpassingly great revelations, there was given me a thorn in my flesh, a messenger of Satan, to torment me. Three times I pleaded with the Lord to take it away from me. But he said to me, "My grace is sufficient for you, for my power is made perfect in weakness." Therefore I will boast all the more gladly about my weaknesses, so that Christ's power may rest on me. That is why, for Christ's sake, I delight in weaknesses, in insults, in hardships, in persecutions, in difficulties. For when I am weak, then I am strong.
>
> 2 Corinthians 12:1–10 NIV1984

First, note that Paul was given this "thorn" to keep him from "becoming conceited because of these surpassingly great revelations" (verse 7). Few of us have had such surpassingly great revelations that we were not even sure if we were in or out of our bodies at the time. Thus, we are hardly candidates to receive a "thorn" like Paul's to keep us from becoming conceited.

Second, Paul calls his thorn a "messenger from Satan" (verse 7). This would be a very odd reference to sickness or disease. A better explanation for the term *messenger* in this passage would be a person, fallen angel or demon who carried a message from Satan. This would fit well if Paul is dealing in this passage with the Judaisers from Jerusalem. These Judaisers may have referred to themselves in such a way that Paul calls them "super apostles" (not meaning it as a flattering term). They also had made critical remarks against Paul that would have been humbling.

Third, of the few references to thorns in the Old Testament, the only three that refer to thorns in the body do not refer to sickness at all, but to human enemies. That makes it even more likely that Paul's thorn in the flesh, which has so often been interpreted as physical sickness or disease, is in fact referring to a person or persons. Two of these Old Testament passages refer to thorns in the side, and one to thorns in the eye, so perhaps that is why Paul chose to say "thorn in the flesh," which would take people's minds back to all three references:

> But if you do not drive out the inhabitants of the land, those you allow to remain will become barbs in your eyes and *thorns in your sides*. They will give you trouble in the land where you will live.
>
> Numbers 33:55, emphasis added

> Then you may be sure that the LORD your God will no longer drive out these nations before you. Instead, they will become snares and traps for you, whips on your backs and *thorns in*

your eyes, until you perish from this good land, which the LORD your God has given you.

Joshua 23:13, emphasis added

Now therefore I tell you that I will not drive them out before you; they will be *[thorns] in your sides* and their gods will be a snare to you.

Judges 2:3 NIV1984, emphasis added

These verses make it clear that the thorn referenced in Paul's Bible, the Old Testament, represented not sickness but people—specifically adversaries. Having once been a leading rabbi, Paul would have known this because he would have had great knowledge of the Old Testament.

This interpretation of Paul's "thorn in the flesh" is not my opinion alone. Many commentators agree with this position, as well as several healing ministers and revivalists such as F. F. Bosworth, Michael Brown and others.[1] In light of this interpretation, for people to think that Paul's thorn refers to sickness and to think that they also might have such a thorn is theological rubble that stands in the way of their healing.

2

An Overemphasis on Sovereignty

One generation shall laud your *works* to another,
and shall declare your *mighty acts*. . . . All your
faithful shall bless you. They shall speak of the glory
of your kingdom, and tell of your *power*, to make
known to all people your *mighty deeds.*

Psalm 145:4, 10–12 NRSV, emphasis added

What has the Church believed about healing, especially in light
of what Scripture says in James 5:14–16? Let's look at that
passage:

Is anyone among you sick? Let them call the elders of the church
to pray over them and anoint them with oil in the name of the
Lord. And the prayer offered in faith will make the sick person
well; the Lord will raise them up. If they have sinned, they will
be forgiven. Therefore confess your sins to each other and pray
for each other so that you may be healed. The prayer of a righteous person is powerful and effective.

Is that what the Church believes and follows? From the beginning of their existence until now, the Orthodox Churches have maintained a belief in healing. They have a liturgical service for healing, and they have a sacrament of healing. And until the tenth century, the Roman Catholic Church had a sacramental rite for the purpose of physical healing. In the tenth century this rite was switched to Extreme Unction or Last Rites, the purpose of which no longer was to bring healing, but rather to prepare a person's soul for death. During Vatican II the Catholic Church restored this sacrament to its former purpose, that of bringing healing to the persons anointed, not primarily of preparing them for death.

Church history reveals that overall, the Church's beliefs about healing and sickness have undergone a great change that is rooted in a fundamental worldview change. For the first eight hundred to one thousand years of Church history, the Church held on to a "warfare" worldview. The Church was at war, fighting against the devil, his demons and disease. This Church's warfare worldview was gradually replaced, however, by a new worldview called the "blueprint" worldview.[1]

Much of the Church's theology of healing has become intertwined with this issue of worldview. Dr. Gregory Boyd has helped us understand the problem of evil (theodicy) not only in relationship to worldview, but also in relationship to the atonement.[2] (Theodicy is the branch of theology that attempts to answer the questions of why a good God permits the manifestation of evil.) Boyd has helped us understand the reality of our struggle against the forces that are opposed to God.[3] If we have a warfare worldview, we expect that bad things may happen to good people because there is a war, and there is no Geneva Convention to regulate the warfare. Satan and his cohorts, principalities, powers, rulers and demons are terrorists. They attack civilians, and there are casualties in war.

This warfare worldview is quite a distinction from the more current blueprint worldview, where everything happens according to the will of God. The blueprint worldview builds upon an overemphasis on God's sovereignty. Because the blueprint worldview sees everything that happens as God's will, it finds it problematic when bad things happen to good people. It also fails to provide believers with the motivation to fight against bad things like sickness and disease. The warfare worldview, however, sees bad things as resulting from the devil and his demons. When bad things happen, it is due to the spiritual warfare people find themselves in.

We can clearly see the outcome of these two worldviews in the area of healing. In the warfare worldview, which was the early Church's position for approximately its first one thousand years, when sickness or disease comes we are to resist it, fight it, pray against it and draw upon the mighty army of God's angels to help us in the battle.

If, on the other hand, we hold to the blueprint worldview—which has been the Church's position for nearly the past one thousand years—instead of fighting sickness, we reason as to why God has allowed it to come upon us. We ask ourselves what good God is working through our sickness or disease. We acquiesce. We don't fight, lest we find ourselves fighting against the hand of God, who supposedly brought or allowed the issue to come upon us in the first place.

We can see the effects of the blueprint worldview on healing in the advice ministers of the Anglican Communion are given about their visitation of the sick. In the Book of Common Prayer of the Church of England, we find the English Office of the Visitation of the Sick, which reveals the sixteenth-century Protestant view of sickness better than any other document. In his book *Healing and Christianity*, Morton Kelsey, an Episcopal priest, professor of religion and author, quotes the

Office's instruction to ministers (emphasis added by Kelsey throughout):

> When any person is sick, notice shall be given thereof to the Minister of the Parish; who coming into the sick person's house, shall say . . . "Hear us, Almighty and most merciful God and Saviour; extend thy accustomed goodness to this thy servant who is grieved with sickness. . . . Sanctify, we beseech thee, *this thy fatherly correction to him; that the sense of his weakness may add strength to his faith, and seriousness to his repentance:* That if it shall be thy good pleasure to restore him to his former health, he may lead the residue of his life in thy fear, and to thy glory; or *else give him grace so to take thy visitation, that, after this painful life is ended,* he may dwell with thee in life everlasting; through Jesus Christ our Lord."[4]

Kelsey comments that the following exhortation was then read—perhaps to a person dying of cancer or a man watching his sick child suffer. If the person was too sick to comprehend more, that is where the reading would stop. If not, there was more of the same to follow. Starting with the statement that almighty God is the Lord of life and death, the exhortation continued,

> "*Whatsoever your sickness is, know you certainly that it is God's visitation.* And for what cause soever this sickness is sent unto you; *whether it be to try your patience for the example of others, and that your faith may be found in the day of the Lord laudable, glorious, and honourable,* to the increase of glory and endless felicity; *or else it be sent unto you to correct and amend in you whatsoever doth offend the eyes of your heavenly Father;* know you certainly, that if you truly repent you of your sins, and bear your sickness patiently . . . and *render unto him humble thanks for his fatherly visitation,* submitting yourself wholly unto his will, it shall turn to your profit, and help you forward in the right way that leadeth unto everlasting life."[5]

In a footnote to the above, Kelsey records some material from the *Visitatio Infirmorum*, an eight-hundred-page volume for clergy that deals with how to visit the sick. It directs that penitential psalms should be read, and it addresses how to conduct services and counsel the sick, especially in regard to issues of faith and morality. What follows is from "The Trial and Examination of the Soul" on pages 499–513 of that large volume:

> Are you persuaded that your present sickness is sent unto you by Almighty GOD? . . . And that all which you now suffer is far less than you have deserved to suffer? . . . Are you fully sensible and convinced now, how little there is in (all your possessions), and how soon you may be, or are like to be taken from them?[6]

Kelsey notes that there was little to cause a sick person to expect healing as a result of this service, only to be comforted and receive strength. But I find little in these words to either comfort me or to give me strength.

Is it little wonder that after five hundred years of such types of teaching in the historical Protestant churches, it is harder for a person who has been taught such theology to receive healing than for a totally unchurched person? This is an example of blueprint theology's impact on the doctrine of healing.

During the past several decades, however, several serious challenges have been raised against this blueprint worldview of reality. The Arminianism that began around 1608 with the *Remonstrance* document was one such early challenge within Protestantism.[7] The *Remonstrance* challenged the blueprint understanding of sovereignty that would make up part of the thought of Augustine, Aquinas and especially Calvin.[8]

Today, not just Arminianism, but also Open Theism[9] and Process Theology[10] challenge the blueprint worldview. Open Theism is the belief that God allows human freedom to reject His plan and will, and that God does not override our freedom.

That obviously conflicts with the blueprint worldview that God controls all things. Process Theology is the belief that God never uses coercion to accomplish His plan or will, and it suggests an understanding that God is in even less control than Open Theism teaches. That also obviously challenges the blueprint worldview.

While I do not believe in Process Theology and I have mixed feelings about Open Theism, still, the blueprint worldview is one we must challenge if believers are going to have faith for their healing. With its overemphasis on God's sovereignty, this blueprint worldview is rubble that we must clear away so we can build up an atmosphere of faith and realize a breakthrough in healings and miracles.

3

The Big Lie about Faith

I will come praising the *mighty deeds* of the Lord
GOD, I will praise your righteousness, yours alone.

O God, from my youth you have taught me, and
I still proclaim your *wondrous deeds*. So even to
old age and gray hairs, O God, do not forsake me,
until I proclaim your might to all the generations to
come. Your *power* and your righteousness, O God,
reach the high heavens.

You who have done *great things*, O God, who
is like you?

Psalm 71:16–19 NRSV, emphasis added

The Big Lie about faith is that *faith that is not dependent on
signs and wonders is superior to faith that is dependent on them.*
This is another example of the theological rubble we need to
clear away in the process of creating an atmosphere conducive
to a healing breakthrough.

I heard this Big Lie often while in college. I majored and
minored in religious studies, and I took all my elective courses

in religious studies as well. Doing that exposed me to a perversion of faith and a travesty of scriptural exposition that supported a liberal, strongly anti-supernatural understanding of Christianity. Many times, I heard my professors emphasize two particular passages from the gospel of John to support their stance. Based on John 20:29 and John 4:48, they taught that faith that was dependent on miracles or signs and wonders was inferior to faith that came about by hearing the Gospel and believing.

Let's start clearing away this rubble by looking more closely at John 4:48 in context:

> Once more he visited Cana in Galilee, where he had turned the water into wine. And there was a certain royal official whose son lay sick at Capernaum. When this man heard that Jesus had arrived in Galilee from Judea, he went to him and begged him to come and heal his son, who was close to death.
>
> "Unless you people see signs and wonders," Jesus told him, "you will never believe."
>
> The royal official said, "Sir, come down before my child dies."
>
> "Go," Jesus replied, "your son will live."
>
> The man took Jesus at his word and departed. While he was still on the way, his servants met him with the news that his boy was living. When he inquired as to the time when his son got better, they said to him, "Yesterday, at one in the afternoon, the fever left him."
>
> Then the father realized that this was the exact time at which Jesus had said to him, "Your son will live." So he and his whole household believed.
>
> John 4:46–53

We do not have to read Jesus' words in verse 48, "Unless you people see signs and wonders, you will never believe," from a negative perspective. The exact same words can be read with either a harsh tone or a sympathetic tone. Jesus understood the importance of signs and wonders to faith, and He even told His audience that if they could not believe in Him because of His words, they should believe because of what He had done—His signs and wonders. As He said in John 10:37–38, "Do not believe me unless I do the works of my Father. But if I do them, even though you do not believe me, believe the works, that you may know and understand that the Father is in me, and I in the Father."

John's gospel records only seven signs out of the many that Jesus performed. In the majority of these passages, the result of the sign was that people came to faith in Christ. John the evangelist, as he is often called, even says, "Jesus performed many other signs in the presence of his disciples, which are not recorded in this book. But these are written *that you may believe* that Jesus is the Messiah, the Son of God, and that by believing you may have life in his name" (John 20:30–31, emphasis added).

The John 4:46–53 passage we have already looked at reveals that the end result of the sign Jesus performed was that the man and his whole household believed. That has to be the best possible result, so if John meant to put a low value on signs and wonders in this passage, he did a poor job of communicating it. In most of John's passages dealing with a sign, his word choice associates the sign with bringing people to faith. The sole exception to this is the third sign he records, the healing of the crippled man at the pool of Bethesda who had been paralyzed for 38 years (see John 5). Rather than emphasizing that people believed in Jesus due to the sign, this story emphasizes the lack of faith on the part of the Jewish leaders, in spite of Jesus' miracles. It indicates that a resulting judgment would be upon them for their failure to believe after witnessing the sign.

My mentor for the doctoral program at United Theological Seminary, Dr. Jon Ruthven, showed in his writings and lectures that signs and wonders are emphasized throughout Scripture. As demonstrations of God's power that act as a basis for faith, they are emphasized not just in the gospels and the book of Acts, but throughout the entirety of the Bible. This is the very opposite of the negative view many liberals hold—the Big Lie that denigrates the value of a faith connected to signs and wonders.

When one considers that out of all the signs Jesus performed, the Holy Spirit guided John to mention only seven, I think it is significant that six of those seven lead to faith. Added to that, the sole exception leads to judgment for not coming to faith after witnessing the sign. It therefore seems ludicrous to me to suggest that the apostle John had a negative view of a faith that was based on witnessing supernatural signs.

How anyone could believe this Big Lie is hard for me to comprehend, yet most liberal schools hold to it. What need does a liberal scholar have that drives or motivates this lie? The need to explain away all the supernatural aspects of the Bible. The liberal pastor or scholar holds to a worldview in which the miraculous is impossible. Stories about miracles are viewed as either legendary embellishments or mythological tales used to teach a theological truth, but having no historical reality.

The apostle Paul is not embarrassed about connecting faith to the supernatural power of God in healings, miracles and signs and wonders. In Romans 15:18–19 he states,

> I will not venture to speak of anything except what Christ has accomplished through me in leading the Gentiles to obey God by what I have said and done—by the power of signs and wonders, through the power of the Spirit of God. So from Jerusalem all the way around to Illyricum, I have fully proclaimed the gospel of Christ.

Paul wrote to the Corinthians, "My message and my preaching were not with wise and persuasive words, but with a demonstration of the Spirit's power, so that your faith might not rest on human wisdom, but on God's power" (1 Corinthians 2:4–5). He also wrote, "For the kingdom of God is not a matter of talk but of power" (1 Corinthians 4:20).

To the church at Thessalonica Paul wrote, "Our gospel came to you not simply with words but also with power, with the Holy Spirit and deep conviction" (1 Thessalonians 1:5). In his second letter to the church at Thessalonica he wrote, "We constantly pray for you, that our God may count you worthy of his calling, and that by his power he may fulfill every good purpose of yours and every act prompted by your faith" (2 Thessalonians 1:11 NIV1984).

The writer of the book of Hebrews was not ashamed of a faith related to signs and wonders, writing, "This salvation, which was first announced by the Lord, was confirmed to us by those who heard him. God also testified to it by signs, wonders and various miracles, and gifts of the Holy Spirit distributed according to his will" (Hebrews 2:3–4 NIV1984).

In addition to the hermeneutical issues of interpretation surrounding the Big Lie, there is the historical issue presented by Ramsay MacMullen, the Dunham Professor Emeritus of History and Classics at Yale University until 1993. He emphasized that the primary reason people came to faith in Jesus during the first four hundred years of Christianity was because of the signs, wonders, healings and deliverances worked by those in the early Church.[1]

Finally, in addition to the hermeneutical and historical issues, there is the missiological issue. While I will not elaborate on this in great detail here, see my book *Supernatural Missions: The Impact of the Supernatural on World Missions* (Global Awakening, 2012) for more on this important issue.[2] Even today, the existential truth for almost all Muslims who are turning to Christ is that they accept Jesus not through great preaching or the great apologetical reasoning of the evangelists, but rather because they first have witnessed something supernatural, usually a healing or miracle (though often also a dream or vision of Jesus).[3]

In summary, the evidence from the Bible, Church history and the mission field reveals how important a role healing, deliverance and miracles play in bringing people to faith. The quality of a faith related to the supernatural is not in any way inferior to a faith that comes through hearing the preaching of the Gospel without signs following it. As part of removing the rubble that stands in the way of a healing breakthrough, it is time for us to put the Big Lie to rest and return to a more biblical rather than philosophical faith.

4

Harmful Hype

I will meditate on *all your work*, and muse on *your mighty deeds*. Your way, O God, is holy. What god is so great as our God? You are the God who works wonders; you have displayed *your might* among the peoples. With *your strong arm* you redeemed your people.

Psalm 77:12–14 NRSV, emphasis added

Some years ago I was at a meeting with my young adult daughter. From the stage the evangelist was waving his arms and yelling, "There is such a powerful anointing of the Holy Spirit in this meeting!"

I looked at my daughter and told her, "We must be in a different meeting."

The presence of God was not powerful in that moment, yet the evangelist continued making declarations about the power of the Holy Spirit's presence.

I again turned to my daughter and said, "This is what you call hype."

What do I mean by "hype"? I define it as publicly announcing that God is doing something when, in fact, He is not. Hyping a meeting is making declarations about how present God is, how powerful His presence is and how He is touching people, when actually, He is not.

Usually, some degree of revving people up emotionally is associated with hype. I remember speaking in a large church that had several score of thousands in its membership, with over ten thousand people present in the meeting. After I spoke, one of the associate pastors took the mic and began to rev up the people's emotions. Becoming quite loud, he was making declarations about what God was doing in the meeting. This grieved me. This pastor did not like the quiet way in which I was ministering healing without hype after I finished speaking. He surely thought I needed help. I did not, and neither did God.

Years before that, I was at one of my first nontraditional meetings for healing (a charismatic meeting). There was such a coordinated effort between the pastor and the worship team to rev things up that it amounted to hype. After a testimony of healing there would be very loud, almost deafening music accompanied by very loud, intense praise. One might even say it was worked-up praise and worship rather than a spontaneous response on the crowd's part. I did not like such hype then, and I still do not like it now.

Why is hype detrimental to creating an atmosphere of faith for healing, especially when the hype is used purposefully to create what the perpetrator hopes will be faith? I believe that over time, hype causes people not to trust you or not to believe that what you are saying is true. This loss of integrity or believability is detrimental to healing ministry.

Trust is extremely important, and trust is built by being truthful. Don't exaggerate your testimony, and don't speak "evangelastically." In the same way as elastic stretches, speaking "evangelastically" refers to stretching the truth. Sadly, some evangelists do stretch the truth. Not all evangelists do this, of course. But enough of them do to make the word *evangelastic* common within the churches. Don't stretch the truth, and don't act spooky or weird. Instead, learn to move naturally in the supernatural.

You don't need hype when you are moving naturally in the supernatural. What do I mean? Let me tell you what I do and don't do so that I move naturally in the supernatural. Here is my list on the *don't* side:

- I don't try to work up people's emotions.
- I don't make exaggerated claims.
- I don't change my voice or use special tactics in an attempt to develop some kind of spiritual climate that is unnatural, spooky or mystical.
- I don't close my eyes and pause for effect or to give the appearance of being super-spiritual.
- I don't do things in a way that we think is okay in church, but that would seem odd outside our church culture.
- I don't feign faith, meaning I am honest when I am unsure whether or not what I am about to say is really God leading me. (The only way to find out is to humbly state my uncertainty, but also state that I desire to obey God in case it is Him.)

Here is my list on the *do* side:

- I do try to be authentic and genuine in my statements and in expressing my feelings.
- I do try to be accountable for prophecies I give to individuals. I ask them if what I said makes sense and whether or not it is true. (I tell them not to be "nice" to me, but to be honest.)

- I do try to explain why I do what I do in a meeting, and I appeal to the people's understanding more than to their emotions.
- I do try to use the language of normal discourse instead of talking in King James English.
- I do try to do things in such a way that they would seem natural if they took place outside of church, even in a business, a restaurant, a school or a hotel lobby.

John Wimber had no tolerance for hype or super-spirituality. In fact, that is one of the reasons I was attracted to him and to the Vineyard in the mid-1980s. When I first came into contact with John, he emphasized making a point of avoiding hype. I want to emphasize it here as well.

5

The Opposite of Hype

We will not hide them . . . ; we will tell to the coming
generation the *glorious deeds* of the LORD, and his
might, and the *wonders* that he has done.

He established a decree in Jacob, and appointed
a law in Israel, which he commanded our ancestors
to teach to their children; that the next generation
might know them, the children yet unborn, and
rise up and tell them to their children, *so that they
should set their hope in God, and not forget the
works* of God . . . and that they should not be like
their ancestors . . . whose spirit was not faithful to
God.

. . . *They forgot what he had done, and the
miracles that he had shown them.*

Psalm 78:4–11 NRSV, emphasis added

False humility is in some ways the opposite of hype. Instead of
saying God is doing something when in reality He is not, this false
humility keeps someone from declaring what God actually has

done or is doing. The result is that the people in the congregation do not hear about what God is doing. This lack of testifying to what is truly happening in the meeting is a terrible impediment to faith for healing. It is fully as detrimental as its opposite, hype, which I talked about in the previous chapter. We must address and correct false humility—clear it away as rubble—if we are to establish an atmosphere that invites a healing breakthrough.

I have heard that speaking in public is the number-one fear most people have. This might explain why people often are hesitant to give their public testimony of what God has done in their lives. But this fear is rooted in pride. We are too proud to speak in public for fear that we might not be good at it. We allow that pride and the fear of failure to keep us from testifying, and then we call it being humble.

Some think we are being prideful when we testify to what God is doing in our lives. But I think being afraid to give our testimony is rooted in false humility. We have to realize that our testimony is not about ourselves but about the Lord, who has done wonderful works in our lives. If given correctly, a testimony does not bring glory to the person healed, but to the Healer—our Triune God, in the name of Jesus.

Once we understand the powerful way in which God uses testimonies, I believe we can push past pride and false humility to give a testimony that brings glory to God. Bringing God glory is one of the results of our testimony. It is a contradiction to sing worship songs like "Glorify Thy Name" and at the same time not give testimonies of His healing in our midst, especially since healing, miracles, signs and wonders are the primary biblical way that God glorifies His name.

God receives glory, honor and praise from people who see or hear about the display of His power in a testimony. The display of His power is a primary way that He reveals His glory. This is revealed in Jesus' Upper Room discourse in John 14–16 and in His high priestly prayer in John 17. These chapters mention glory nine times. In fact, both the apostle John and the apostle Paul use the terms *glory* and *power* synonymously.

The acts of power Jesus, and later His disciples, did by operating in the Holy Spirit's gifts are referred to as fruit in John 15:8: "This is to my Father's glory, that you bear much fruit, showing yourselves to be my disciples." In context, this is the fruit of *doing* that John 14:12–14 refers to:

> Very truly I tell you, whoever believes in me will do the works I have been doing, and they will do even greater things than these, because I am going to the Father. And I will do whatever you ask in my name, so that the Father may be glorified in the Son. You may ask me for anything in my name, and I will do it.

It is not the fruit of *being* that Paul refers to in Galatians 5:22–23: "But the fruit of the Spirit is love, joy, peace, forbearance, kindness, goodness, faithfulness, gentleness and self-control."

These acts of power through the Holy Spirit cause the Triune God to receive glory, and they cause people to put their faith in Jesus and His Gospel. I realize I am repeating myself a little in this section, but I also know this is a big issue—this idea needs repeating in order to bring us the light of truth about healing. Instead of faith being established independent of signs and wonders, the New Testament seems to present a much more favorable understanding of faith that is established by both word and *deed*. We can see this in the seven signs the gospel of John talks about. Let's look at them briefly.

1. The disciples believed in Jesus after He turned water into wine in John 2:1–11: "This, the first of his miraculous signs, Jesus performed at Cana in Galilee. He thus revealed his glory, *and his disciples put their faith in him*" (verse 11 NIV1984, emphasis added).

2. People believed in Jesus after He healed a royal official's son from a distance in John 4:43–54: "Then the father realized that this was the exact time at which Jesus had said to him, 'Your son will live.' *So he and all his household believed*" (verse 53 NIV1984, emphasis added).

3. There is no record that the healing of the man at the Pool of Bethesda in John 5:1–9 caused anyone to come to faith, but this healing is followed by a passage in which Jesus deals with people believing in Him in order to pass from death to life (see John 5:10–47, especially verse 24).

4. Five thousand people believed in Jesus after He multiplied bread and fish to feed them in John 6:1–14: "After the people saw the miraculous sign that Jesus did, they began to say 'Surely this is the Prophet who is to come into the world'" (verse 14 NIV1984). The term *Prophet* here is a messianic title. During the interbiblical period between the Old Testament and New Testament eras, one of the views was that the Messiah would be a Prophet. Another view was that Messiah would be a King, and another was that He would be both Prophet and King.

5. A man born blind believed in Jesus after Jesus healed him in John 9: "Then the man said, '*Lord, I believe*,' and he worshiped him" (verse 38 NIV1984, emphasis added).

6. People believed in Jesus after He raised Lazarus from the dead in John 11: "Therefore many of the Jews who had come to visit Mary, and had seen what Jesus did, *put their faith in him*" (verse 45 NIV1984, emphasis added). Likewise, look what the chief priests and Pharisees were thinking after that miraculous sign: "'What are we accomplishing?' they asked. 'Here is this man performing many miraculous signs. If we let him go on like this, *everyone will believe in him*, and then the Romans will come and

take away both our place and our nation'" (verses 47–48 NIV1984, emphasis added). John 12 also records more fruit of belief from the raising of Lazarus: "Meanwhile a large crowd of Jews found out that Jesus was there and came, not only because of him but also to see Lazarus, whom he had raised from the dead. So the chief priests made plans to kill Lazarus as well, for on account of him *many of the Jews were going over to Jesus and putting their faith in him*" (verses 9–11 NIV1984, emphasis added).

7. Following the resurrection, the disciples put their faith in Jesus again in John 21:1–7, after they miraculously caught so many fish by switching the net to the other side of the boat, as He had instructed them to do: "Then the disciple whom Jesus loved said to Peter, 'It is the Lord!'" (verse 7 NIV1984).

To this day, the Church retells these seven signs from John's gospel as a testimony of Jesus and His miraculous deeds. John adds near the end of his gospel, "Jesus did many other miraculous signs in the presence of his disciples, which are not recorded in this book. But these are written *that you may believe that Jesus is the Christ*, the Son of God, and that by believing you may have life in his name" (John 20:30–31 NIV1984, emphasis added). He also adds, "Jesus did many other things as well. If every one of them were written down, I suppose that even the whole world would not have room for the books that would be written" (John 21:25 NIV1984). Obviously, this statement was intended as hyperbole, yet it indicates the significance of the seven signs John chose to write about, as he was led by the Holy Spirit.

I do not know how the connection between the testimony and people putting their faith in God could be any clearer. Seeing and hearing about the mighty deeds of Jesus brings people to faith and brings glory to God. This was not only true in Jesus' time; *it is still true today*. The testimonies of what Jesus continues to do in and through His Church still bring people to faith and still bring glory to God. These testimonies also create faith for healing—not just salvation.

6

Expecting Too Much
or Not Enough?

> Very truly I tell you, whoever believes in me will
> do the works I have been doing, and they will do
> even greater things than these, because I am going
> to the Father.
>
> John 14:12

Several years ago I was listening to a Christian radio talk show in which the speaker was handling questions about physical healing. He was saying that he believed healing was possible today and that there were gifts of healing, but that healing was not supposed to be normative. Other more theological types responded to his subject by saying that those who expect healing to be normative (as I do) hold to an overrealized eschatology. That simply means that in the present, we are expecting too much to happen that is reserved for the millennium.

Besides the fact that such an understanding is unbiblical, the problem with thinking healing is not normative is that this view becomes self-fulfilling and healing becomes rare instead of regular. Yet for those who believe healing is normative, it becomes just that—regular instead of rare.

As I have stated elsewhere, there was a time in my life when healing was anything but normative. Even after twenty-four years of ministry, healing had not yet become normative for me. It had become much more frequent after the first fourteen years of ministry than it was before, but in the last twenty years healing has become normative. It was not the will of God that changed. The problem was not His sovereignty; the problem was my theology and my expectancy.

The increase in the anointing on my life also was important. Now when I am conducting a meeting where we will be praying for the sick, I actually expect that a minimum of 10 percent of the people will be healed. If it is a better than average meeting, we could see 20 to 30 percent of the people receive a healing.

I want to encourage you to begin to believe that it is God's will for healing to become normative in His Church—and that it is God's will for healing to become normative in the church you attend. Why shouldn't we expect healing every time there is a service that includes healing prayer? Healing was normative for Jesus and His apostolic Church, and it was normative for several hundred years in the early Church.

What about in our time? Are we expecting too much or not enough? If we are in the "not expecting enough" camp, we have some rubble to clear away in order to begin building an atmosphere of faith for a healing breakthrough. I don't believe I have an overrealized eschatology, but rather that my detractors have an underrealized eschatology.

7

The Deception of Cessationism

O give thanks to the LORD, call on his name, make
known his *deeds* among the peoples. Sing to him,
sing praises to him; tell of *all his wonderful works*.
Glory in his holy name; let the hearts of those
who seek the LORD rejoice. Seek the LORD and *his
strength*; seek his presence continually. Remember
the *wonderful works* he has done, *his miracles.*

Psalm 105:1–5 NRSV, emphasis added

I ask you not to tell my friends Drs. Rolland and Heidi Baker,
Dr. Leif Hetland, Bill Johnson, Dr. James Maloney and apostolic leader Henry Madava that there are no healers or
workers of miracles today because the gifts of healing and
miracles have ended. Please don't tell my young associate
evangelists, Will Hart, Paul Martini or Ed Rocha, that the
days of miracles and healings are over. Don't tell the young
biblical scholar Timothy Berry, either, or my former interns
Annie Byrne or Paulos Hanfere. You see, these people don't
know about this news. They are being used—all of them—to

see people being healed on a regular basis. Paulos would be shocked if someone told him the news, because he just conducted crusades in Ethiopia and Tanzania where hundreds were healed in each crusade.

I spent much ink and many pages dealing with this false teaching that the days of healings and miracles are past in the book I wrote with Bill Johnson, *The Essential Guide to Healing* (Chosen, 2011). In the chapter titled "Unbelieving Believers and Believing Unbelievers," I spelled out the theological and biblical reasons to believe in the continuation of healing today. I also dealt with various church and societal issues that are involved in causing some people to have so little faith for healing. I wrote a whole book to refute this particular error of believing the time for healing has come and gone, *The Essential Guide to the Holy Spirit: God's Miraculous Gifts at Work Today* (Destiny Image, 2015).

The big issue, however, is the deception of cessationism. It is taught based on a faulty understanding of the purpose of miracles. This faulty understanding comes from the cessationists' inconsistent historical methodology regarding healing for the biblical and post-biblical periods, and from their failure to apply proper hermeneutical principles to the Bible.

When people understand the correct purpose of miracles—that miracles occur not to accredit correct doctrine, but as an expression of the Gospel of the Kingdom—then the system of cessationism starts to crumble. When people understand that the office gifts listed in Ephesians 4:11 are supposed to exist "until we all reach unity in the faith and in the knowledge of the Son of God and become mature, attaining to the whole measure of the fullness of Christ" (verse 13), then the Church starts clearing away the cessationist rubble. When this text and others are interpreted in light of their context, without a cessationist pretext, then their true meaning indicates that healings and miracles, as well as healers and workers of miracles, were to continue until the return of Jesus.

Also, when we realize the apostles only wrote about half of the New Testament, and that only a few of them wrote any Scripture, we begin to see their role in a different light. If we do not see apostles as primarily the writers of Scripture, then it is not necessary to limit their existence to the first century. If instead, we see apostles as strategic church planters and as fathers of other leaders who have a vision for the Kingdom of God to reach new regions, then that kind of primary apostolic role would necessitate the continued ministry of apostles in the Church until Jesus returns. This appears to have been the role of many of the apostles in the New Testament, even among some of the Twelve. I would maintain that such a role continues in the Church in our day.

It is interesting and ironic to discover that a major text used by cessationists—those who believe the gifts of prophecy, tongues, interpretation of tongues, the working of miracles and the gifts of healings have ended—is the very verse the early Church used to prove that the gifts of prophecy would *not* end until the Second Coming of Jesus. I refer to 1 Corinthians 13:8–10 (NIV 1984):

> Love never fails. But where there are prophecies, they will cease; where there are tongues, they will be stilled; where there is knowledge, it will pass away. For we know in part and we prophesy in part, but when perfection comes, the imperfect disappears.

Many denominations that came out of the Reformation hold to the Protestant teaching that the gifts have ceased, ending with the death of the apostles, their immediate disciples or the canonization of the Bible. This group believes the word *perfection* in this passage is a reference to the Bible being completed. That interpretation could not have made sense to the Corinthians to whom it was written, however, and therefore it violates one of the basic principles of scriptural interpretation. That principle says that the interpretation of a text must allow the text to have made sense to its original hearers.

The rise of Montanism was another factor that added to the confusion surrounding this passage. This sect of early believers felt the Church had become too organized and had lost much of its original power. Led by a man named Montanus, with two prophetesses alongside him, its adherents believed that they were the last generation of Christians before the Second Coming. With this view, they believed that they would be the last of the prophets and that prophecy would cease after them, because Jesus would have returned. The early Church responded to Montanism by quoting 1 Corinthians 13:8 as the basis for believing that the gifts were to continue until the return of Jesus.

Look also at Acts 11:21: "The Lord's hand was with them, and a great number of people believed and turned to the Lord." In context, the apostles had remained in Jerusalem, and it was the new believers who had been driven from the city. It is these new believers who are referenced in the phrase "the Lord's hand was with them." All the gifts were meant to be an expression of the Good News that the Kingdom of God was at hand, that it was within the believers, and that there were times when "the hand of the Lord" was especially with the believers, not just the apostles. Healing was not, then, the sole possession of the apostles; neither was it relegated to them and the first deacon-evangelists like Philip and Stephen. Instead, it was possible then—as it is now—for all believers to experience these manifestations of grace. Scripture uses expressions such as "the Lord's hand was with them" or "the hand of the Lord was upon them" to indicate the power of God coming upon His people—power working deliverance, healing and miracles beyond the natural realm.

8

A Deistic or Liberal Worldview

Note the connection between "word" and "power" in the notion of "testifying" in Acts 4:33: "And with great power the apostles were giving their testimony to the resurrection of the Lord Jesus, and great grace was upon them all." Acts 19:10–12 summarizes Paul's ministry as does the phrase "word and deed" (Rom 15:18, imitating Jesus, Luke 24:19). So also, the characteristic way God reveals himself: "God also bore witness by signs and wonders and various miracles, and gifts of the Holy Spirit distributed according to his will" (Heb 2:4). This is the normal, even exclusive, way that God reveals himself.

Jon Ruthven[1]

Before I ever went to college, where I majored, minored and took all my electives in religious studies, before I ever attended seminary and before I went back to seminary to pursue a doctorate, I had heard seminaries being called *cemeteries*. Why were seminaries often referred to as cemeteries? Because too many students entered them with a lively faith and exited them with a dead faith; too many entered believing in a God who worked miracles and exited convinced that the miracles were not true.

Many seminary students were taught naturalistic explanations for miracles at best, or were taught that miracles were legendary embellishments or myths at worst—liberal theology. Or they were taught that these things occurred during the ministry of the apostles, but ended with the death of the last apostle, or with the death of the apostles' last disciple, or with the canonization of the Bible—the cessationist fundamentalist position.

The real irony of these two positions, the liberal and the fundamentalist, is that they ended up in the same place in regard to modern-day gifts of the Spirit, though for very different theological reasons. Whether proponents of these two positions graduated from the most prestigious divinity schools or from unaccredited Bible institutes, they made strange bedfellows. Neither position would teach its members to expect healing and miracles in the life of the Church today.

Even more ironic, there is more openness on the part of the liberal institutions to having someone come and lecture on healing than there is on the part of the fundamentalist institutions. Why does this happen? It is not for the same reason that the fundamentalists and many evangelicals do not believe in the supernatural. They believe that the Bible is true and the miraculous happened, but that the miracles were only for a time, to get the Church started. They believe that once the Bible was canonized, the miracles were not needed anymore. They believe in the supernatural in the past, but have a deistic understanding more so in the present. Deism proposed a God who created the universe, but who remained removed from it once it was finished. After that, He supposedly remained aloof and uninvolved, allowing the universe to run on the laws He established. He would not have violated those laws to allow for a miracle to happen.

The liberals, on the other hand, are taught a new method of interpreting the Bible, the historical-critical method. It replaces the historical-grammatical method of the fundamentalists, which goes all the way back to the first few centuries of the Church. This was the method of interpretation the school of Antioch embraced. The school at Alexandria would have promoted the allegorical method. The historical-grammatical method insisted that the proper manner of interpreting a Bible text was to do so in a way that was faithful to the meaning of the historical context—the way it would have been understood by its first-century audience, and by the rules of Greek or Hebrew grammar. It rejected the allegorical method.

The liberals' new historical-critical method of interpretation followed the Enlightenment, which was based on the scientific method, using reason and a view of reality that presupposed miracles could not happen and did not happen. Their understanding of the universe's existence was based on the laws of Newtonian physics, which could not be violated by a miracle. To allow for the miraculous would cause a disruption of the existence of the universe. Since a new historical method of research was developed based on this anti-supernatural presupposition, any reports of miracles in history were discounted as legendary or mythological. Within this methodology, miracles could not be accepted as genuine.

I was taught this liberalistic historical-critical method all the way through college, and through earning my master of divinity degree from The Southern Baptist Theological Seminary in Louisville, Kentucky. In my last year of seminary, however, I studied a textbook called *The Historian and the Believer* by Van A. Harvey (MacMillan, 1969). This book was an eye-opener for me. Until I read it, I had not understood that this method of interpreting Scripture was based on an anti-supernatural understanding of reality or presupposition. It all fit together logically, if one held to this anti-supernatural presupposition. But if you did not hold to an anti-supernatural presupposition or worldview, but believed the supernatural is possible today, most of the method's conclusions or interpretations would no longer hold true. I realized that for almost six years, I had been taught an interpretive model that was based on an anti-supernaturalism I did not hold to. With this realization, I was able to clear away the rubble and regain much of the faith that liberalism's skepticism had destroyed in me.

9

"Sickness Is My Cross to Bear"

This sickness will not end in death. No, it is for God's
glory so that God's Son may be glorified through it.

John 11:4

Another piece of rubble we need to remove in order to build
the wall of faith for healing is the view of sickness being a
personal cross to bear. I remember as a child hearing people
say things like, "This sickness is my cross God has chosen me
to bear." Somehow, they thought God had put illness on them.
Usually, they perceived their sickness as either something they
deserved or something with a cause-and-effect relationship to
their lifestyle. Sometimes they saw it as a cross they could bear
to bring glory to God. Sometimes they saw it as the method
God had chosen as a means of sanctifying them.

Dr. Francis MacNutt refuted these arguments in his first
book, *Healing*, which I read in 1976. In his book, he states that
he attended a conference in 1973 in South America about reviv-
ing healing ministries. At this meeting, there were priests and
sisters in attendance who had long worked for social causes. He

recounted that one man, Father Ralph Rogawski, had survived a gunshot attack on the place he was staying. MacNutt reported that at the meeting,

> Christ was once again at work among his people just as he was 2,000 years ago, reaching out to heal the sick and wounded. One missionary reported that nearly 80 percent of the poor people they prayed for in the barrios of Bolivia were cured or notably improved. . . . Like these Catholic missionaries, Protestant missionaries returning to Fuller Seminary in California reported that healings and exorcisms are commonplace and necessary in the Third World.[1]

Throughout his book, MacNutt helped me see that although this belief that "sickness is my cross to bear" is rooted in much popular Catholic thought, it is not a biblical viewpoint, nor is it official Catholic doctrine. That describes what it is not, especially in terms of the Roman Catholic Church. What it is for all of us, in fact, is rubble we must clear away if we are to set an atmosphere of faith and see a healing breakthrough.

After doing a word search for *sick* or *sickness* in the New Testament, I found not one verse that indicated it was a cross to bear. I found not one verse in which sickness was seen in any positive way. The only passage that connected the words *sick* or *sickness* to the glory of God involved Lazarus, whom Jesus raised from the dead after an illness. John 11:1–4 tells us,

> Now a man named Lazarus was sick. He was from Bethany, the village of Mary and her sister Martha. (This Mary, whose brother Lazarus now lay sick, was the same one who poured perfume on the Lord and wiped his feet with her hair.) So the sisters sent word to Jesus, "Lord, the one you love is sick."
>
> When he heard this, Jesus said, "This sickness will not end in death. No, it is for God's glory so that God's Son may be glorified through it."

The passage's implication is that God would receive glory through the events that took place, and that God's Son would be glorified not through Lazarus's sickness, but through his resurrection.

The only passage I found in the New Testament that seemed to connect sickness in any way to something received from God is Revelation 2:21–22, which refers to an immoral woman causing issues in the church in Thyatira. The Lord said of her, "I have given her time to repent of her immorality, but she is unwilling. So I will cast her on a bed of suffering, and I will make those who commit adultery with her suffer intensely, unless they repent of her ways."

In this passage, the suffering is not seen as a cross to bear for the Lord. Rather, it is a judgment from the Lord because of this woman's serious sin, which was affecting others in the local church, and because of her refusal to repent. (See this story in its context to understand how serious this situation was to Jesus. The woman was causing both theological heresy and moral sin in others in her local church.)

Other than that passage in Revelation, I could find nothing in the New Testament that suggested sickness originates from God. I could not find one single passage in the New Testament that backs up the theology that sickness is our cross to carry. When you embrace that kind of poor theology surrounding sickness, it is hard to have faith for healing because you believe God has brought on you whatever the issue is that you are suffering from. It is difficult to ask God to remove it if you believe He gave it to you in the first place. That is why it is so important to clear away this particular rubble, which puts an obstacle in the way of people's faith for healing.

10

Mistaking Emotionalism for Faith

The commands to announce the kingdom through healings and deliverances represented the very core of Jesus' own ministry that the disciples, as disciples, were replicating. This Spirit-centered charismatic mission was also commanded in Acts 1, and what was demonstrated throughout the rest of Acts and the epistles.

Jon Ruthven[1]

God made our bodies and said they were good. I don't hold to a gnostic type of Christian faith that is concerned only about the soul, caring nothing about the body. God also made us as emotional beings. There is nothing wrong with experiencing or expressing our emotions. But it is a detriment to our faith to believe we must work up our emotions in order for God to respond to our prayers. In chapter 4 about hype, we talked a little about this in the sense of a minister or leader trying to rev up a crowd. Let's look at it on a personal level here.

In my Baptist church in southern Illinois, during what was the most powerful meeting of my life up to that point, I witnessed Blaine Cook shush the crowd to lower their volume.

"Calm down, calm down," Blaine told the people. "You don't have to work up your emotions to be touched by God."

Actually, working up your emotions can get in the way of being able to know or hear what God is doing. Many times in Brazil, it has felt like the emotionalism in a meeting was taking over and the people were working themselves up into a frenzy. In such situations I have often tried to explain to the people that this is unnecessary and can even make it harder to recognize what God is doing.

If you are working your emotions into a high-pitched state, it is harder to notice whether or not God is beginning to touch you physically. It is also harder to know whether the Holy Spirit is speaking to you. If He is speaking in a still, small voice, your overworked emotions make it harder to hear Him. Better to dial down the emotions and listen.

This is not to say that there is no place for emotions. For example, it is unnatural not to express emotions—even strong emotions—when the Holy Spirit is touching you in conversion, or when you are baptized in the Spirit, or after God has just healed you or the person you are praying for. In these cases, not feeling elated with joy, thanksgiving and praise would be abnormal to our human makeup. Sometimes your emotions will run the gamut from great joy you might express in laughter to such love that you are overwhelmed by God's goodness and weep uncontrollably. And sometimes the emotion you feel is such deep peace that all you can do is lie in His presence, perhaps having lost your ability to move or to rise up from the floor.

Heidi Baker experienced all these emotions in Toronto when I gave her a prophetic word that was accompanied by a fresh filling or baptism of the Holy Spirit. Heidi and her husband, Rolland, are missionaries in Mozambique. I first met them in 1997 when they were looking for a divine touch from God. They came to Toronto in 1996 when Heidi was quite ill. They were touched there, and Heidi was completely healed. In 1997 they returned, and during my message Heidi left her seat to come to the altar. She looked at me, and I could see that she was crying. I spoke a word about Mozambique to her—that God was going to give her that nation. I told her, "You are going to see the dumb speak, the lame walk, the blind see and the dead be raised."[2]

The power of God suddenly came on Heidi in that moment. She felt both heat and electricity, and she experienced both laughter and tears. A little while later, she could not even move from the neck down. It was the most powerful experience with the Holy Spirit that Heidi had ever had. Out of this experience came the Bakers' great faith for Mozambique and an even stronger anointing for winning that nation.

This was the most powerful experience of the Spirit that Heidi had ever had in her life. It was the most intense and the longest in duration, lasting seven days and nights. It also bore the greatest fruit. When some people saw Heidi in her state of helplessness and often drunkenness in the Holy Spirit, they laughed at her, thinking it was funny. But Heidi told me that it was not funny at all; it was actually very scary to be so utterly undone by the Spirit of God. It was also a genuine move on God's part, not worked-up emotionalism on her part.

Let me tell you another story that will encourage your faith and hunger for a greater baptism in the Holy Spirit. This story also involves a person's emotions that came as a response to what God was doing, not as worked-up emotionalism mistaken for faith. This story and Heidi's are not meant to show the only way God empowers someone, but to show only one way God can and does affect people. And if God can do it for others, then don't you think He can do it for you? I want to encourage you to press in for more intimacy with God. Press in for a greater experience of His power, which will result in more effective evangelism on your part.

This story happened to my former worship leader at the St. Louis Vineyard Church, Bob Balassi. He is a highly educated, successful businessman and is the CTO/VP of a company he helped build. As a technology executive who works in the secular field, Bob is not prone to emotion. In fact, he is quite the analytical type. Yet Bob's baptism in the Holy Spirit is one of the most inspiring stories I have heard.

One day, Bob left work, feeling sick with the stomach flu. His wife and three young children were also sick with it. Bob arrived home to a house filled with vomiting chaos. As he was hugging the commode himself, he said a short prayer asking God to heal his family. Thinking to himself that God could heal everyone in the home with just a blink of His eye, Bob felt his hands and face suddenly begin to tingle. Then they were electrified, and he felt as if his fingers were going to blow off.

At that point, as if lifted into the heavenly realm, Bob began to experience a whole gamut of emotions and to sense the awesomeness of God's attributes—His incredible love, righteousness, power, holiness, majesty, splendor, etc. He was laughing and then crying as he experienced each incredible wave of God's character and glory. Kathleen, his wife, came into the bathroom with the three children. She sat there with the toddlers in her lap, observing her husband being baptized and overwhelmed with the Holy Spirit. Praise and petitions filled his mouth. The Lord instructed him to pray, right there in the bathroom, for Kathleen and his children. Each of them was healed along with Bob, and the chaos returned to peace.[3]

Saint Augustine experienced a conviction and conversion himself. His book *The Confessions of Saint Augustine* clearly shows that he ran the gamut of emotions, too, as he experienced more of God. He relates that at one point the Lord was turning him around so he could see himself, and it was a "foul sight: crooked, filthy, spotted, and ulcerous."[4] He describes his emotional reaction this way:

> I saw and was horrified, and I had nowhere to go to escape from myself. . . . You were setting me in front of myself, forcing me to look into my own face, so that I might see my sin and hate it. . . . Now the day had come when in my own eyes I was stripped naked and my conscience cried out against me. . . . I was being gnawed at inside . . . lost and overwhelmed in a terrible kind of shame.[5]

Following that harrowing experience, he "lashed his soul with every scourge of condemnation . . . flung himself down on the ground under a fig tree, and gave free rein to his tears."[6] Obviously, he was experiencing strong, deep emotions in response to the conviction of the Holy Spirit. Then he heard a voice constantly repeating, "Take it and read it. Take it and read it."[7]

Augustine stopped his tears, rose up and began to read silently the words of the apostle Paul: "Not in rioting and drunkenness, not in chambering and wantonness, not in strife and in envying, but put ye on the Lord Jesus Christ, and make not provision for the flesh in concupiscence."[8] At the end of this sentence, Augustine's heart was "filled with a light of confidence and all the shadows of doubt were swept away."[9] His emotions had changed entirely, and in that moment, "The conversion of St. Augustine, of his intellect which could not resist the truth, and of his will which could resist the good, was accomplished."[10]

I experienced something similar to Augustine in my conversion, which took me through a wide range of emotions, all the way from godly sorrow under conviction to great joy and peace. I am not against emotions; at the time of my conversion I was already weeping from the conviction of the Holy Spirit. When I knelt to pray, ask forgiveness for my sins and surrender my life to God, the depth of my weeping increased. And like Augustine, the moment I prayed through, the moment I knew I had been saved, the moment of my conversion, I was no longer filled with sorrow and grief over my sinful state. Instead, I was filled with peace, filled with joy and filled with love.

When I was baptized in the Holy Spirit, I was unable to stand on three occasions, but able to stand on another occasion. On all these occasions I was aware of great love flooding my soul. I was in tears during all but one occasion. I was aware of a tremendous peace during one occasion. On two occasions there was tremendous heat, and I experienced the sensation of an electrical current going through my body.[11]

Obviously, in telling you all this I have proven that I definitely am not against experiencing emotions in the presence of God and in response to what He is doing. At the same time, however, I am sensitive to when emotions are appropriate and when they are an impediment to the work of God. When it comes to receiving healing or being filled with the Holy Spirit, let's not mistake emotionalism for faith. It is better to wait in peace, neither trying to control your emotions nor work them up. Instead, simply embrace whatever God is doing in that moment.

Overreaction to the "Word of Faith" Position

We are commanded to use that divine power (*ischuos*) in Eph 1:19 and 6:10, which appears in the context to be the normative, characteristic miracle power of the Spirit-filled Christian.

Jon Ruthven[1]

While I was in seminary, I visited a Catholic prayer group and a Southern Baptist charismatic church. I also read a lot about the charismatic movement, as well as doing some writing on the subject. As a result, I graduated from seminary with a positive perspective on the movement. It would not take long, however, before my perspective changed.

What brought about my reversal from a positive view to a negative view of the charismatic movement? It came about because of my introduction to a very unbalanced representation of the Word of Faith movement in southern Illinois. Before I go further, I want to say that my experience should not be considered normal, nor was it fair to the Word of Faith movement. But for years, the only representatives of this movement that I was exposed to were poor representatives.

While pastoring in southern Illinois, I met some Word of Faith pastors and some members of their churches. I spoke on Christian television programs where the other speakers were Word of Faith people. I also had multiple experiences with former members of Word of Faith churches, people who had been wounded by the poor representation of the movement in their churches. Often, these wounded people told me that they had been afraid even to admit that they had a physical need and request prayer, because some in their Word of Faith circles perceived this as a negative confession. The problem was that many people in their churches saw an honest confession of need, whether for healing or other things, as detrimental to having that need met. They maintained that Christians should only make positive confessions. This introduced a fear of praying more than once for a need, because they believed that to pray again indicated a lack of faith in the first prayer.

On one occasion I remember speaking on a local Christian television station and then meeting the other speaker and his wife afterward, who were both Word of Faith people. The station representative took us all to lunch afterward.

"You know, Jesus wasn't poor; He was blessed," the other speaker began to tell me during our meal. "Jesus had lots of resources."

The man was wearing a Rolex watch, and he and his wife had arrived at the station in a fine car. Those things were not why this guy turned me off, however. The way that he equated having these things with God's favor and blessing turned me off. I think things like that *could* be evidence of God's blessing and favor, but the problem is in assuming that unless you own a Rolex, a fine car or a large home, somehow you are falling short and are not as spiritual as those who do possess them.

It got me thinking about how the Bible informs us in Luke 2:22–24 that the offering Jesus' parents made for their newborn son in the form of two doves was an offering that the poor could give. I also was thinking of the many other scriptural indications that Jesus was not wealthy, but poor. He even stated, "Blessed are you who are poor" (Luke 6:20). And I was thinking of people I know of whom God has used for great healings—even for raising the dead—who do not even own a watch or a car and who live in a mud hut.

As a result of the experiences I had with those who were not the best representatives of the Word of Faith movement, I developed a prejudiced, negative view that extended even to the charismatic movement as a whole. Later this viewpoint, which was more of a prejudice or judgment on my part, would change. What brought about the change? Bill Johnson introduced me to Pastor Joe McIntyre while I was in Seattle. Bill also gave me Joe's book, *E. W. Kenyon and His Message of Faith: The True Story* (Empowering Grace Ministries, 2010). This well-documented, well-researched book helped me understand that Kenyon and the Word of Faith movement were not influenced, as many believe, by New Thought or Christian Science. Rather, the influence came from the Faith Cure movement, which in turn had been influenced primarily by the Holiness movement, especially the teaching of Hannah Whitall Smith and the "shorter way" to experience sanctification that she espoused.[2]

Kenyon was most influenced by Baptist pastor A. J. Gordon, under whose preaching he had been rededicated. I learned that while Kenyon had attended Emerson College, which would become a hotbed for New Thought, he had only been there for one semester, during the time that he was backslidden. He took courses in oratory at Emerson, intending to become an actor. Ralph Waldo

Trine, the Emerson professor noted for New Thought teaching, had not yet started teaching those views while Kenyon attended there.[3] So not only was Kenyon *not* influenced by New Thought; I learned that he was even opposed to its teaching. I also learned that he was a Baptist who had the heart of an evangelist.

Joe McIntyre helped me understand the true roots of the Word of Faith movement. He told me about a meeting Kenneth Hagin had with Word of Faith leadership where he rebuked the movement most associated with his name for making its emphasis too materialistic rather than spiritual. Hagin announced at that meeting that he was about to release a book called *The Midas Touch: A Balanced Approach to Biblical Prosperity* (HAGN, 2012), in which he would attempt to bring some balance to the movement.

Joe also told me about many good representatives of Word of Faith teaching, including some well-balanced pastors of large churches. In addition to Joe's influence, about two decades ago God began to surround me with people who were in the Word of Faith movement whenever I would go to major conferences. As we introduced ourselves to each other, I would end up hearing their testimonies of how God had healed them. Often, these healings were from terminal conditions and these people were healed through believing for their healings.

In Florida, one of the women seated next to me shared how she had been healed of cancer as she confessed her healing. A man seated next to us was a missionary whose whole family served with him in Nicaragua. He shared how his wife had come back to the orphanage one time to discover that a young child had died in her absence. She took the child in her arms and went out and sat on the ground, declaring life over the child. The child was raised from the dead.

Through all this I discovered that there was not just a negative picture of the Word of Faith movement; there was also a positive picture. Whether or not you came away with a positive perspective depended on the representatives you met. Then I read Dr. Paul King's book *Only Believe: Examining the Origin and Development of Classic and Contemporary Word of Faith Theologies* (Word & Spirit Press, 2008), which looks at both the arguments of the critics and the position of the Faith Cure and Word of Faith movements. Dr. King evaluates which group is most correct, the critics or those within the movements. He discovered that the critics are usually the ones most in the wrong in their positions. This confirmed for me that I had been too negative in my evaluation of the Word of Faith movement.

Finally, as I traveled the world I became aware that the impact of Word of Faith teaching could be positive. I developed a new perspective on this when I saw the benefit Word of Faith teaching could have on people who are marginalized, oppressed or without hope. Those who are stuck in hopelessness by a deterministic sense of never being able to escape or improve their lot in life need the positive message Word of Faith can bring.

Word of Faith teaching can be very positive for people born and raised in hopeless contexts around the world. Slum dwellers in America, favela dwellers in Brazil, barrio dwellers in Argentina, garbage dump dwellers in Mozambique or in the Philippines—all grow up in hopelessness. They usually don't have parents like mine, who told me I was as good and as smart as any doctors' or lawyers' kids. They told me that if I got an education, I could become anything I wanted. My mother told me over and over that I could be anything I wanted, and that I was as smart as any other kids at my school. She believed I could escape the limitations of my family's history. Because of her, I knew I could be the first Clark in my family to go past the eighth grade, and that I could become somebody.

Other children in my small community were not told that they could escape from the limitations they grew up under. Some of them are still living in situations where their income is well below the national median and they are working at dead-end jobs. Either they did not escape, or they chose not to escape. Like them, many people in the poorest situations in the world feel hopelessly locked in poverty. The Word of Faith's positive message—that God wants people to prosper in every way, including economically—is so important to combating a sense of determinism that locks the poor into hopelessness. Word of Faith brings a message of hope to such people. This message— that God is concerned about blessing and prospering them, and that all things are possible for them—helps them fight depression, despair and a sense of determinism.

Helen Thompson's story is an example of this, although it is not a story about economic hope, but about hope for healing. Helen and her husband, Bill, were the first couple to commit to DeAnne and me when we started the St. Louis Vineyard. The two of them were present for all the teachings on healing I gave as pastor. Helen was present at almost every conference we held. Prior to meeting us, she had already been well grounded in Scripture and in her faith. She was present when we brought in many men and women who had a strong anointing for healing.

About 25 years after the times we shared at the Vineyard church, I had a chance to speak with Helen and reflect back on those days. She said she had always struggled with different health problems during that time period and had never been called out by a word of knowledge for her physical conditions. She had never been healed through the laying on of hands by any of the visiting healers at our church. She told me that all she had left was her hope in the promises of Scripture for healing. Without that hope, she said she would have been overcome by deep depression due to her diseases.

This trust in Scripture's promises for healing that Helen displayed has been the position of the Word of Faith movement.

The Vineyard movement in some ways was the antithesis of the Word of Faith movement. The Vineyard's emphasis is more on the gifting of God, recognizing what the Father is doing, and dependence on the Holy Spirit. The Word of Faith is more about trusting, believing and confessing the promises of Scriptures; people come into a faith where healing comes as they possess what they have confessed. The emphasis in Word of Faith is on the quality of people's faith and their ability to have faith. The emphasis in the Vineyard is on God's gift of faith, or even on His ability to give information that causes people's measure of faith to rise.

I had planted the first Vineyard church in the St. Louis area and the second one in Missouri, as well as the first one in Illinois. Now, almost two and a half decades later, as I spoke on the phone with Helen she told me that all she had left to keep her from despair was teaching similar to that of the Word of Faith movement. That says something for its validity.

Another validation that the Word of Faith movement has more merit to it than most people outside of it are willing to admit came while I was studying for my doctoral thesis. I ran across a statement by Dr. Herbert Benson, a professor of medicine at Harvard University, that was amazingly positive in regard to healing through what he called "cognitive restructuring." This term is a more sophisticated way of saying "confession-possession," a major theme of the Word of Faith movement. Dr. Benson wrote,

> Wonderfully, humans already have a custom-installed device that filters information we receive and that can be empowered to heal us. This device is your belief system—the thoughts, feelings, and values that are unique to you and your life experience. Our minds are conditioned to react in certain ways, the wiring of our brains formed when we repeatedly call upon particular

memories or thoughts and their signature neurons and neuron combinations.

Because the brain is ever-changing, we have the ability to rewire and modify those automatic reactions in a process sometimes called "cognitive restructuring." . . . Because of the brain's intrinsic malleability, you have the opportunity to literally "change your mind."

In all the activities I am about to recommend, the goal is not to deny reality, only to project images and ideas of something better for yourself. You act "as if" the preferred reality were true and the body responds. . . . By acting as if our bodies are invincible in the ways I'll prescribe greater health can emerge. . . . After saying something enough times, we start to believe it.[4]

Dr. Benson has much to say about faith and cognitive restructuring. He is limited in his understanding, however, in that he limits the effects to the natural and denies the supernatural. Yet he does lend credence to the value of positive confession, and the Word of Faith perspective is related to positive confession.

Some kinds of healing are dependent on the truth emphasized in the Word of Faith movement's teaching. Other healings are dependent on the truths emphasized in other streams of the Christian healing river.[5] Both emphases have their value.

I have done my best to make amends for my former negativity about the Word of Faith movement. Whether this has been out of penance or out of a desire to make up for the many negative judgments and statements I made in the past, I am not sure. Perhaps it resulted from the time I visited Rhema Bible Church and was so profoundly touched by evangelist Rodney Howard-Browne. During that visit I heard the Holy Spirit speak to me internally, saying, *I love these people, and I don't like your attitude toward them. Look how much they love Me. Many of them have left their careers to come here and prepare to pastor. I want you to quit being angry toward them.*

Shortly after having this impression, I went to the Word of Faith movement leaders who were present and asked them to forgive me for speaking badly against them. (At the time I thought it was only my attitude that was wrong. Later, I discovered that some of my theology and perceptions were also wrong.) I have since made positive statements in regard to the value of some of the Word of Faith teaching. I also have created another four-day school through Global Awakening, with twenty-four teachings on the subject of *Faith and Healing.* I invited Pastor Joe McIntyre, who oversees hundreds of Word of Faith pastors, to join my executive director, Tom Jones, and me in teaching this new school. I also invited Dr. Paul King, who was a professor at Oral Roberts University for years and has both a D.Min. and D.Th. degree. I invited Dr. King because I was greatly impressed with his aforementioned book, *Only Believe: Examining the Origin and Development of Classic and Contemporary Word of Faith Theologies.*

In essence, while some of my past experiences with certain Word of Faith proponents turned me off to the movement, I have come to realize that judging the movement as a whole based on these incidents was an overreaction on my part. That kind of negativity is rubble we need to clear away so that we can acknowledge the positive things about the Word of Faith position. That in turn can help us set an atmosphere for healing, especially where words of knowledge have not been given, or where there have not been opportunities to receive prayer by ministers well-known for their anointing in healing, or where healing has not come after such prayers.

12

Leaving the Rubble Behind

> You performed miraculous signs and wonders in
> Egypt and have continued them to this day, both
> in Israel and among all mankind, and have gained
> the renown that is still yours.
>
> Jeremiah 32:20 NIV 1984

To summarize, what have we learned so far about creating an atmosphere that invites a healing breakthrough? We have discovered that in order to build the wall of healing in the Church, a wall that has in many ways crumbled, we must do two important things: build an atmosphere of faith for healing and repent of our faulty belief systems. To ready ourselves to create that atmosphere of faith, we first need to clear away the false teaching, or what I have been calling the rubble, of several positions that have become part of many people's belief systems. We need to cast into the sea of forgetfulness beliefs that hinder faith, beliefs that encourage skepticism and beliefs that explain away healing, never bringing them up in our minds again. We need to repent of such belief systems.

The Greek word for repent, *metanoia*, literally means to change the way we are thinking. In what ways do we need to change our thinking? That is what part I of this book has been all about. In each of the previous eleven chapters, we looked at some specific rubble that we must clear away. As a sort of checklist to help you complete that process, let's quickly review the various pieces that make up that rubble.

First, we need to acknowledge that there is good reason to believe that Paul's thorn in the flesh was not a disease or sickness, but actually represented opposition from other people. We also need to see that this thorn was given to keep Paul from becoming too proud over his heavenly revelation or visitation—and few of us ever need to worry about having the kind of heavenly visitations and revelations that Paul did.

Second, we need to recognize that for too long, we have attributed the lack of healing and miracles we see to God's sovereignty instead of to our loss of faith, holiness and purity in the Church. We must take note that when we change our expectations, the percentage of people we see being healed also changes, and many more are healed than before. This fact points out that it was not God's sovereignty that was the issue, but rather our lack of understanding regarding healing. Our poor, inadequate theology was the problem.

Third, we need to realize that the attack on faith related to or based on healing and miracles should come to an end. A faith independent of the miraculous is not a superior faith. We need to recognize that according to John's gospel, faith is almost always seen in connection to some sign, healing or miracle. The negative view against connecting faith to the supernatural is based on liberal, anti-supernatural beliefs, not on the clear teaching of scriptural text.

Fourth, to maintain integrity and trustworthiness we need to avoid all hype or exaggeration in our claims. How can those who are ministering expect people to believe their reports when they are making exaggerated claims all the time? They talk (often rather loudly) in certain moments about how God's power is manifestly with them, when clearly He is not as profoundly present as they say. It damages their credibility, along with damaging the atmosphere they are trying to build for healing.

Fifth, we need to avoid the opposite of hype, false humility. We cannot allow ourselves to be intimidated about honestly acknowledging what God is doing in our midst and in our services. We must come to understand the high degree of importance that the Bible itself puts on the testimony, and we must speak out about the great things He is doing.

Sixth, we need to abandon the belief that it is the will of God that healing be non-normative. We need to replace that with the belief that God desires healing to be the normative experience of the Church. In other words, we need to replace our low expectations with higher expectations. Healing was normative in Jesus' ministry. Healing was normative in the life of the apostolic Church, as recorded in the book of Acts and the letters of the apostle Paul. Healing was quite normative in the first three hundred years of the Church. Today, for much of the Church around the world, healing has become normative once again.

Seventh, we must abandon cessationism because it is based on several key misunderstandings. It incorrectly understands the purpose of miracles; they were not given simply to accredit correct doctrine, but rather as part of the Gospel or the Good News of the inbreak of the Kingdom. Cessationism also applies an inconsistent historical methodology and a flawed biblical hermeneutic, resulting in several key issues within the position, such as ignoring the role of the Holy Spirit beyond salvation and ignoring many passages in the New Testament that would support a continuationist view of the gifts. And finally, cessationism ignores the fact that healings, miracles and other gifts of the Spirit are occurring all over the world today—evidence so great that no one truly can ignore it or explain it away.

Eighth, we must realize that a deistic, liberal worldview is not a biblical worldview. We must reject it not only as denying the clear teaching of Scripture, but also as denying the clear experience of the Church today. Many professing Christians must wake up to the fact that they live their lives like deists instead of theists. I do not believe the deistic interpretation of Christianity, wherein the Creator does not personally involve Himself with those He created, is orthodox. I believe it is heretical. Yet many people live the lifestyle of a deist, even while claiming to embrace a theology of theism, wherein God cares for and involves Himself with His creation.

Ninth, we must reject the teaching that sickness is our "cross to bear." The scriptural passages that portray suffering in a redemptive, positive light are referring to persecution and hardship for the sake of the Gospel, not to sickness. For years, many commentators have read into these texts physical suffering from sickness and disease, whereas actually the texts refer to persecution and tribulation.

Tenth, we must have a psychological and biblical understanding of emotions. We can believe there is a sound, healthy, biblical place for emotions in our spiritual lives, while also limiting undue excess. We need to avoid the fear of emotion that lies behind the use of the terms *enthusiasts* or *enthusiasm* in a negative connotation, while at the same time avoiding emotionalism based on the belief that such is necessary in order to move God to work on our behalf. Although it is reasonable to express gratitude and joy when He does move (in fact, it would be odd if we did not), His move does not depend on the heights or depths of our emotions.

And lastly, number eleven on our list of things to clear away in the theological rubble, we ought not throw the baby out with the bath water when it comes to the teaching of the Word of Faith movement. We ought not allow the ad hominen arguments about a few of its representatives, which create what can be seen as a ridiculous straw man, to persuade us that this straw man is a faithful representation of the best teachers in the Word of Faith movement.

Now that we have done some hard work clearing away the rubble that we needed to remove, I will give much more attention to the subject of faith in part II just ahead. There we will turn our focus in a new direction, leaving behind the rubble and concentrating instead on what we can do to build up a solid wall of faith so that more healing and miracles will occur. Let's now go on to examine the specific things we can put in place to create an atmosphere of faith for seeing a healing breakthrough.

PART II

Building a Wall of Faith
for a Healing Breakthrough

"As for me, this is my covenant with them," says the
LORD. "My Spirit, who is on you, and my words
that I have put in your mouth will not depart from
your mouth, or from the mouths of your children,
or from the mouths of their descendants from this
time on and forever," says the LORD.

Isaiah 59:21 NIV1984

You are about to begin part II of *The Healing Breakthrough*,
and I am excited for what you are about to learn. In my own
life, when I learned how to relate faith to spoken words that
came from the leading of the Holy Spirit, it was a huge leap
forward in my healing ministry. We will start building a wall
of faith for healing with this subject, the connection of spoken
words to faith. We will look at how such words encourage the
faith of both the person who is ministering healing and the
person who is being prayed for.

From there, we will move into how to receive these insights and directives from the Holy Spirit. We will also consider how important it is to understand the ways of God and how much that understanding facilitates the ministry of healing. I will also talk about how to recognize the ways of God. Once you become aware of His ways, it will help you have more faith for your own healing or for someone else's.

Moving on from these practical matters, we will look at the nature of faith itself. We will consider several ways that the word *faith* is used in the New Testament and talk about its various meanings. I also want to tell you about six variables that I studied closely in my doctoral thesis research. Each of the six variables can have an impact on the probability of seeing more people healed.

Then there is the subject of contending for healing. Sometimes it takes determination along with faith! And other times, as much as we contend for healing, some of our prayers go unanswered. Handling those unanswered prayers and guarding against the discouragement and disappointment that can accompany them are the subject of another chapter. I talk about what to do when the answer you have hoped and believed for does not come. It is an inevitable reality of healing ministry that we will have to face at some point, as some of my examples from people's lives will show.

Whether you are the one in need of prayer for healing, or whether you want to see more people healed when you pray for them, the chapters in this part of the book will benefit you. They address very practical matters having to do with the heart of healing and its relationship to faith. Underlining this part of the book is the reality of our co-laboring with God to build a wall of faith for a healing breakthrough.

13

Back to Seminary at 59

Study to shew thyself approved unto God, a work-
man that needeth not to be ashamed, rightly divid-
ing the word of truth.

2 Timothy 2:15 KJV

I was 59 when I began a doctor of ministry program. You may
ask yourself, *Why would someone go back to school at such
an age?* It is a good question, especially since I did not need
another degree to enhance what I was doing. I was ministering
over two hundred days a year already and could not accept all
the invitations I was receiving.

Why did I go back to school then? I believed that many unbiblical beliefs were making their way into the Church, where
they were causing confusion and weakening the Body of Christ.
I wanted to help stop that erosion of the truth, and since it had
been 33 years since I had graduated with my master of divinity degree, I felt as though I needed to hone up on my biblical
studies and theology to do that most effectively. I also wanted to
gather others to go through further training with me. I wanted

to raise the bar, so to speak, regarding the training of key leaders whom I hoped to work with in the future.

A second reason I went back to seminary was that I was becoming more aware of the importance of verifying Christian healing. I realized that not only did I need to know how to better communicate what I believed; I also needed to know how to bring evidence of healing. I went back to school with two goals about that in mind: First, I planned to garner evidence about the kinds of healing that were occurring. Second, I wanted to discover what could increase the likelihood of a healing occurring.

Initial Attempts at Schooling

My first attempt to get a doctorate was through the South African Theological Seminary. I was accepted into the program, but I did not think the professor who was to oversee my doctoral work and dissertation was a good match for me. He was not in the school of theology but in pastoral care, and he specialized in counseling. I had hoped to have Dr. Jon Ruthven or Dr. Gary Greig as my overseer because both had written wonderful dissertations and books more closely related to the field of study I wanted to write about, the supernatural, particularly the continuation of the gifts of the Spirit today.

I had paid my full tuition for the entire program up front, however, so I started preparing by reading books on writing my thesis. Then suddenly, I was hit with excruciating pain. I soon found out I had what doctors call classic traveler's back. It involves losing the lower lumbar lordosis (curve of the spine) so that the lumbar is flat instead of curved. It also involves indescribable discomfort!

For the next ninety days, I could not sit in a chair; neither could I stand up without crutches. My pain was so bad that I was on four different prescriptions, including Percocet, a powerful pain reliever. All I could do during those ninety days was lie on a mat. I used crutches anytime I had to stand. The pain was terrible.

I found out that my condition had resulted in three herniated disks and two pinched nerves. My shin felt as if it were in a vise grip, and the side of my hip and my knee both felt as if they had been shot with a rifle. The physical therapist I was seeing, who had a doctorate in his field, told me that if I did not end up having surgery I would become the poster child for physical therapy.

I learned a lot about physical therapy while going six days a week for ninety days. I learned that you test for improvement by means of a visual analysis score (VAS) test, a mobility test and a range of motion measurement. The VAS test scores pain levels on a scale of 0–10, with 0 representing no pain and 10 representing excruciating pain. Patients report their pain levels when they are admitted to the program, and then every few weeks the physical therapist asks them the same questions they were asked at the beginning to determine whether or not the treatment is being successful. This is an important test for insurance companies, which use it to determine whether or not they will continue paying for a patient's treatment.

In addition to a patient's self-evaluation of pain, there is also the mobility test. The physical therapist looks at your posture and how you carry yourself to see if you are compensating for pain through the way you stand and move. There is also the range of motion test, done with a simple device that tests the angle you can move an arm or leg. All these tests are used to determine whether or not physical therapy is helping with your healing.

After ninety days, I still was not doing so well on the tests. I still was in a lot of pain (though it was less pain), I could not walk without crutches, and I was unable to function. This was a scary time for me and for the fifty employees who depend on my being able to travel and minister to raise the money necessary to cover their salaries and the other costs of the ministry. I went ahead and did a healing school while on crutches. During this time, a journalist from Canada wanted to do a report on me. I allowed it, and years later I accidentally found a Canadian TV show that selectively used his footage. The coverage was negative, stating that there was one person I could not heal—myself. I wish that TV company had followed up with me, because before the program aired I had already been healed.

How was I healed? The first part of the healing came through my son Josh. He called me on Skype from Japan while I was lying in great pain on the floor. Josh prayed a powerful prayer on my behalf for healing. Immediately, the 24/7 pain left. For the first time since the onslaught of the problem, I was without pain.

The healing was not complete, however. Yes, the constant pain had stopped, but I could not put any weight on my left foot without sharp pain coming into my leg. If I took the pressure off the foot, the pain would stop. A few weeks later I went to bed after setting my crutches off to the side. I still could not put any weight on my left foot without sharp pain. When I woke up the next morning, I accidentally touched my foot to the floor while reaching for my crutches. To my surprise, I felt no pain. I stood up—still no pain. I walked without the crutches—no pain. I went around the corner to see if I could climb the stairs normally, which I could.

I shouted to my wife, DeAnne, "I've been healed! I don't know how it happened, but I've been healed!"

That afternoon about five hours later, I received an email from Ray Smith, a friend near Baton Rouge, Louisiana. He wrote me about a bizarre experience he had in a worship service on the previous night. He said he saw me in a vision, and at one point my clothes, skin and muscles disappeared. He was left looking at my spinal and neurological system. In the vision he heard the Lord tell him to take his finger and push the material that had come out from my three ruptured disks back into the disks. He obeyed, acting out what he was seeing in the vision. He told me the people around him must have thought he was crazy because of the way he was acting.

I called Ray immediately and told him, "It was the Lord! You really did see and hear from the Lord, because I've been healed in my sleep." We were both elated over his bizarre vision that resulted in my healing.

Because of the timing of my intense back issue, I decided not to go on with my work toward a doctorate through South African Theological Seminary. The other thing that factored into my decision was being unable to have the mentors or overseers I felt were the best fit with what I wanted to write about.

Sometime later, I found a seminary on the East Coast that seemed like a good possibility. They would allow me to use Dr. Ruthven as my doctoral advisor or overseer. By this time I knew exactly what I wanted to write about as the subject of my dissertation. I had been healed myself, and I had begun to see people with surgically implanted material in their bodies regain a wide range of motion and have their pain disappear as a result of prayer. I wanted that to be my topic. Some of my friends in academia mentioned to me, however, that the accreditation of this East Coast seminary was only regional, not national, and that I should try to get a degree from a seminary accredited by the U.S. Department of Education. For the second time, I put my seminary plans on hold.

School Again at Last

I was preaching in Ann Arbor, Michigan, at a Vineyard church when I met a Korean American, Dr. Andrew Sung Park. He approached and told me three times in our conversation that he had been surprised when he had heard me speak. My curiosity got the best of me, and I asked him why he was surprised and specifically what it was that had surprised him. He told me that although he was a professor at a United Methodist seminary, I had taught him some things. He was shocked by the fact that I had good theology. He asked me about my background and schooling, and I told him I had a master of divinity degree from The Southern Baptist Theological Seminary in Louisville, Kentucky.

Dr. Park then told me that he believed what I was teaching needed to be taught at the seminary level, and that if I would come to United Theological Seminary he would give me a full scholarship. He also told me that he had looked at my book *There Is More* and that it was written well enough to be the basis for my thesis. This meant I would not have to do much more writing to complete my thesis. (This was the version of the book before I had it published with a major publisher, who revised its academic tone and trimmed some wording to broaden its readership.)

I thought I might get bored using that approach, however, and I wanted instead to research something new—the effectiveness of prayer on people whose bodies contained surgically implanted materials that resulted in them suffering chronic pain or loss of range of motion. I wanted to first prove that such people were being healed in my meetings, and then I wanted to study six variables that might impact the probability of all kinds of healing occurring. Some of these variables are the building blocks we will talk about in the chapters ahead. They are things that I believe—and that my research shows—will help you build an atmosphere of faith to usher in a healing breakthrough.

I told Dr. Park that I would only accept his offer if the seminary would also give a scholarship to my executive director and friend, Tom Jones, and if the seminary would agree to allow Dr. Jon Ruthven to become my thesis mentor and advisor. Long story short, the seminary agreed to all my requests and I finally was able to pursue my next degree.

Breakthrough Research into Healing

Once my research and writing were complete, Dr. Andrew Sung Park, Dr. Jon Ruthven, Dr. Gary Greig and Dr. Luther O'Connor were the examining committee for my thesis. Dr. Park commented that it was a very important thesis, breaking into new ground. He said it was a breakthrough in research because it crossed over into the medical field, as well as including the theological field, and he added that he knew of no other thesis in any seminary that had done anything similar.[1] That had been one of the very reasons I wanted to do the research I had in mind for my dissertation. I wanted to provide solid evidence of healing to encourage further medical studies. I realized that in order to impact the medical field, we needed to provide evidence of healing.

I believed my thesis would be beneficial in promoting further research in both the theological and the medical fields. Such research would combat New Age healing modalities like Reiki and Therapeutic Touch, on which some medical studies have already been done. The result of those medical studies has been that these methods have found more favor in the medical field, even to the point that their practitioners are able to receive insurance monies for their treatments in some areas of the United States.

As a result of my studies in the doctoral program at United Theological Seminary and as a result of my research, I discovered the insights I will share in the rest of these pages about how to create an atmosphere of faith for healing. Of course, their discovery was also based on my experiences in praying for people in more than 11,000 meetings, not only during the year I spent conducting my studies for writing my thesis, but also over the course of my healing ministry. I pray that these insights will help you build a solid wall of faith for healing in yourself and others.

14

Relating Spoken Words to Faith

It is written: "I believed; therefore I have spoken."
Since we have that same spirit of faith, we also believe and therefore speak.

2 Corinthians 4:13

I was on my way from our hotel to an amazing Baptist church
in Mauá in Brazil, a city about an hour from São Paulo. The
first time we had visited this church, it was a little white block
building on the wrong side of the tracks and had only a couple
hundred members. While en route this time, I was meditating
on what had happened there on our first visit. The pastor had
been desperate for God's touch back then and had become
open to the gifts of the Holy Spirit. A great release of healing
had taken place. People from other churches had attended that
initial meeting, packing the little church's facility to overflowing.
They were healed in the sanctuary, healed in the halls and even
healed outside the windows, where they were listening in the
churchyard. We had seen deliverances and all kinds of healing
take place, even of genetic issues and incurable diseases.

I thought we were at the wrong church the second time we visited, because we did not go across the tracks to the little white block building. This time the church was located on a main thoroughfare in the city, and its sanctuary seated 2,200 people. But during the second visit the place was also packed. I will never forget all the miracles we saw on our second visit. In my meetings elsewhere after our second visit, I showed a short video of testimonies about some of the healings that had taken place at that church. What follows is only a small sample of those testimonies, but many more healings occurred during that four-day visit than I can describe here.[1]

Two women who had been totally blind in their right eyes from birth were healed.

Doctors had told a teenager that they would have to amputate her leg due to a cancerous bone tumor, but the girl was healed.

A man had been in excruciating pain from recent back surgery that had involved implanting two metal bars and four screws. He heard the word of knowledge for healing of people with metal in their bodies, and he started doing backbends, bending over to touch the floor, and jumping up and down. Only a few minutes before, he had been in such excruciating pain that he could not sit any longer. It also hurt him to stand up, so he was about to leave the meeting. Just before he left the building, he heard that word and was healed.

A woman with complications from polio was healed.

Two women with cancer in their breasts were healed by a word of knowledge.

A woman who came with her arm in a cast from severe tendonitis heard a word of knowledge about someone wearing a cast. She knew it was for her and believed, and her pain left. She went out and cut off the cast, and then she brought it to the front while giving her testimony.

A man who had lost the cartilage in his knees over twenty years before was totally healed and received a creative miracle.

Another man had experienced pain in his feet for twelve years; it would come suddenly out of nowhere. He also had been unable to kneel due to pain in his knees. At the meeting he experienced the opposite of what he was used to—all the pain in his feet left. He started jumping up and down on his feet, and then he knelt down because he realized the pain in his knees also was gone.

In preparation for our third visit, I had told the team that even though our trip was fourteen days long and included four different cities, the greatest meetings would take place at that church. I also told them I had purposefully set this city as our last place of ministry so that we would end the trip with the most powerful meetings. When we got there, my team and I were not at all disappointed.

During our third visit I was told that the reason those who were healed one night were not coming back the next night was because the church had now grown to 9,000 people. Since we were only scheduled on four nights, the pastor had divided the congregation into fourths and had told everyone that they could come only on their designated night. That way, others would be able to attend when it was their turn. Each night 2,200 people (or about a quarter of his congregation) came, which filled the church to capacity. During these meetings we saw many healings and some miracles. I was amazed at how this church had grown.

A Few Key Life Verses

En route to the church on that third visit, I had an impression: *In Jesus Christ, it is not yes and no, but yes.* I could not remember where this verse was in the Bible, but thanks to an iPhone app I found it quickly in 2 Corinthians 1:19. I had never spoken on it before, but I felt I was supposed to do so, including the expanded text from verses 18–20. I had not prepared notes on it, of course, so I felt inadequate. But clearly the Lord wanted me to speak on this passage. I also felt I was to join it to 2 Corinthians 4:13 for the complete message.

I obeyed, and an amazing outpouring of the Holy Spirit resulted, with many healings. That night I prayed for a young man in his twenties who was deaf in his right ear and paralyzed on his left side. A brain aneurysm had burst while he was having surgery, causing both of his issues. I watched as this young man received healing. I prayed for him for over an hour, and gradually more and more use and feeling came back to his left side. He was wearing thin nylon workout clothes, and at first I could feel the coldness of his muscles. As I was praying, the cold began to grow warm. This was followed by feeling coming back into his muscles, which was followed by the restoration of his ability to move his left arm and then leg. The last thing healed was his deaf ear, but before the night was over he was able to hear out of it.

The passages I preached on that night became my life verses for the next several years. I don't know how to explain their importance to me, but they became huge in my life. I want to unpack them for you here so that you, too, will begin to make the connection between declaring your faith and seeing power released. I learned that it is important not just to believe that God is about to do something, but to declare or state what it is you believe He will do. When you speak that out in front of a congregation, it shifts the atmosphere of faith because your spoken words are related to building the people's faith.

The Holy Spirit has quickened several passages to me that are keys to building faith in order to experience more healings.

The Scriptures I talked about that night at the church in Brazil are among them. Let's examine those two more closely, 2 Corinthians 1:18–20 and 2 Corinthians 4:13, along with one other verse I will add, Revelation 19:10. These are the main passages that deal with the relationship between speaking and faith.[2] Look at the passages themselves, and then we will examine their context and application.

In 2 Corinthians 1:18–20 (NIV1984), Paul writes,

> But as surely as God is faithful, our message to you is not "Yes" and "No." For the Son of God, Jesus Christ, who was preached among you by me and Silas and Timothy, was not "Yes" and "No," but in him it has always been "Yes." For no matter how many promises God has made, they are "Yes" in Christ. And so through him the "Amen" is spoken by us to the glory of God.

In 2 Corinthians 4:13 (NIV1984) Paul writes,

> It is written: "I believed; therefore I have spoken." With that same spirit of faith we also believe and therefore speak.

And in Revelation 19:10 (NIV1984) John writes,

> For the testimony of Jesus is the spirit of prophecy.

Let's look at the context and application of these passages one at a time.

Context and Application, 2 Corinthians 1:18–20

The context of this first passage involves Paul being accused of unfaithfulness to his word because he did not come to Corinth as planned. Paul explains why he did not come, and he says that although his plans did not work out, his gospel was always faithful. He states, "For no matter how many promises God has made, they are 'Yes' in Christ. And so through him the 'Amen' is spoken by us to the glory of God" (2 Corinthians 1:20). This verse emphasizes the principle that the promises of God are yes in Christ, and that believers are to agree by speaking a congregational amen to the glory of God. This is applicable to our topic here.

When it comes to application, all three of these passages have caused me to realize that it helps create faith in a meeting when the ministers or leaders speak out what they believe God has indicated He will do, or what they honestly believe is going to happen. In this first passage, the emphasis is on the promises in Christ being yes, not yes and no. In addition, it states that we speak the amen to the glory of God. The congregation must realize that the amen is to a specific promise, such as a word of knowledge that is a *rhema* word from the Holy Spirit. Because we are one Body it is important that the people speak the amen in their hearts, even if the revelatory word is not for them. Their response of faith, represented in their heart-spoken amen, releases the power of God for healing and miracles, which in turn brings glory to God. I believe if the truth of these verses could grip a congregation so that we moved from an individual to a corporate understanding of their application, a major breakthrough would result in our churches—including a healing breakthrough.

Context and Application, 2 Corinthians 4:13

The context of this second passage involves Paul and the apostles suffering for the Gospel. Paul identifies with the psalmist and quotes Psalm 116:10, where David said, "I trusted in the LORD when I said, 'I am greatly afflicted,'" and then went on to express faith in the midst of his affliction. Paul's context is similar, and the couple of verses following our key verse point to confidence and hope in the resurrection, and also to the growing apostolic work of evangelizing more and more people—which causes thanksgiving to overflow to the glory of God (see 2 Corinthians 4:14–15). I think that since Paul does not finish the quote from David about his affliction, perhaps he does not want to limit the quote's application to affliction. Rather, he may want to expand it to speaking in faith in a more general sense, because the principle of speaking out being related to faith is applicable to more than being faithful in suffering.

In application, this second passage relates believing to speaking. Faith is seen as hearing from God and then declaring what God has communicated. Paul called this speaking with the spirit of faith. He states, "With that same spirit of faith we also believe and therefore speak." Notice that the word *therefore* is related to believing by the spirit of faith. The question to ask is, what is the source of this faith? Does it arise within our human capacity, or does it come by grace as a "gracelet," or a gift from God? The answer is that it comes as gift!

Context and Application, Revelation 19:10

The context of this third passage involves the statement of the angel who appears to John on the island of Patmos. When John falls at his feet to worship him, the angel says, "Do not do it! I am a fellow servant with you and with your brothers who hold to the testimony of Jesus. Worship God! For the testimony of Jesus is the spirit of prophecy" (Revelation 19:10 NIV1984). The spirit of prophecy is concerned with the testimony of Jesus. And the testimony of Jesus is the spirit of prophecy. I believe it is hermeneutically correct to say, "The testimony of what Jesus has done prophesies to what He can and will do." It bears witness or testimony to the mighty works of Jesus. As prophecy is to build up and encourage, as well as to comfort, the testimonies of Jesus act as prophetic words to encourage, build up and comfort those who need a mighty deed done in their bodies by the power of His name and prayer in His name.

As far as application, in Revelation 19:10 John has just been warned by the angel not to worship him since he is a fellow servant with John and with those who hold to the testimony of Jesus. Then the angel tells John, "For the testimony of Jesus is the spirit of prophecy." What does this mean? In the Old Testament there was the word of God and the testimony of God. There were the commandments of God and the testimony of God. Bill Johnson first pointed out to me that when the people of God forgot the testimony of God, they began to backslide. This testimony consisted of the mighty deeds God had done among them.[3] Perhaps this is how *testimony* is being used in Revelation. It is telling others what Jesus has done—His mighty deeds. Or it could be telling the Gospel, which includes both mighty deeds and words. Another consideration is the way in which we should understand the word *prophecy* here. Again, Bill Johnson notes that one of the more subtle functions of prophecy is to carry with it an invitation. Prophecy invites a repetition of God doing again what is being spoken out prophetically.[4]

The Relationship between the Gifts

The late John Wimber and the late Omar Cabrera were most instrumental in helping me discover the ways of God regarding revelatory gifts. They helped me understand how these gifts can occur, and they also showed me how to instruct the crowds regarding these gifts to build their faith. It is a matter of teaching the people the relationship between the gifts of revelation and the gifts of power.

Just to be clear, let me mention that the gifts of revelation are words of knowledge, words of wisdom and the discerning of spirits. The gifts of power are healings, faith and the working of miracles. The gifts of speech are prophecy, tongues and the interpretation of tongues. This division of the nine gifts into three categories containing three gifts each is quite normal in Pentecostal and charismatic churches, although I now question whether it would be more accurate to add prophecy to the revelatory gifts category.

Omar Cabrera also taught me the importance of understanding the role of the angelic realm in healing and the importance of asking God to send the angels into a meeting. He shared with me how the angelic would manifest to him, and he taught me how he knew how to interpret what he saw, thus creating faith inside himself to see the greatest miracles of his crusades. Further, he taught me how to teach on words of knowledge to build people's faith.

Through his associates, John Wimber indirectly taught me how to recognize words of knowledge. They were teaching others what John had taught them, especially Blaine Cook in my case. I also learned from John's writings, and from his direct teaching when he allowed me to shadow him in 1984 and 1985 at his meetings in the United States. In this way, I learned how to recognize signs of God's presence.

My experience is important in that through it I have gained insight into how gifts, faith, and healing and miracles are related. These insights come from 45 years of experience in ministry, with 30 years of actively praying for the sick. I also have had occasion to work and dialogue with more than a dozen ministers who are all noted for their ministry of healing.[5] During these years of ministering to thousands of people in several thousand meetings, I noticed the connection between healing and faith, and the connection between faith and revelatory gifts. With few exceptions, most of the miracles involved a gift of faith, and almost always this gift of faith was the result of a revelatory gift. Even when it seemed no gift such as a word of knowledge or a prophecy occurred, there was the "still, small voice," or an impression instructing either the person praying or the one being prayed for about what to do.

For example, two of the greatest healings I know of took place where no apparent word of knowledge was involved, yet where revelation was involved. One was the healing of a woman from the United States who had paranoid schizophrenia, anorexia and severe obsessive compulsive disorder. The other was the healing of a man from Brazil who was totally blind for over fifty years due to a muriatic acid spill. This man had no visible pupils or corneas; all you could see in his eyes was thick, white scar tissue.

The woman was healed when a relative heard an impression, *Go get her and bring her to the meeting.* He did so, and in that meeting her healing began and was finished during the night. The woman herself also heard an impression after she got home, *Anoint your head with oil*, and she obeyed. Then she heard another impression, *Now anoint your whole body with oil*. Again she obeyed. This time the power of God came as an electrical force knocking her to the floor, where she lay all night with currents of electricity going through her body. In the morning she was healed.

The blind man was healed when a woman on my ministry team heard an impression, *Pray for him*. At five years of age he had spilled muriatic acid in his eyes, which had resulted in his complete blindness for over fifty years. Instead of beautiful brown Hispanic eyes, both of his eyes were covered by about an eighth of an inch of white scar tissue. The woman on my team prayed for him for five hours. Whenever she would stop to interview him, though, she would find out nothing was happening.

How could she pray for five hours when nothing was happening? It was because she kept having the strong impression, *Do not stop praying*. She obeyed, not stopping until it was time to leave the meeting. At that point there had been no change in his ability to see. The woman returned to the United States the next day, unaware of any changes in his condition. On the third morning following the meeting, however, the man woke up without any scar tissue! He also had new pupils and corneas, and good vision.

These cases, however, would not be normative. The norm would be for a prophecy or word of knowledge to precede the faith to sustain the prayer. Moreover, though no public word of knowledge or prophecy was given in these two cases, the two people most involved in the healings both had a personal revelation about what to do. One of the ways you can receive a word of knowledge is through an impression, which is what happened in both cases.

Laying a Foundation with Words

Another insight into the relationship between the spoken word and faith is that the type of healings you talk about in a meeting usually increases the incidence of those healings occurring. Here I refer specifically to healing testimonies shared by video, but we should not limit this to video testimonies alone. It is also true that what you share can change the atmosphere concerning people's faith or expectation. For example, you can build an expectation in the people for healing with what you share before a video and with what you share before giving words of knowledge.

If you tell the congregation that they can be healed by watching the video—even without hands being laid on them and even without being prayed for from the platform—then people often experience healing while watching the video. If you show the same video without making that statement regarding healing, however, usually no one is healed while watching the video. This reveals that healings are not limited by the sovereignty of God, but rather by the expectation of those watching.

In like manner, if you give words of knowledge without first laying a foundation, then fewer people are healed. You have to lay the foundation for people to understand how words of knowledge reveal the will of God and how they can be healed by a word of knowledge without anyone praying for them. And if you take time to explain the purpose of words of knowledge— that they reveal specifically what it is God wants to heal—then many more are healed.

People who do not understand these things do not receive healing when a word of knowledge is called out for them, because they have no concept of the relationship between words of knowledge and healing. In contrast, you see an almost universal experience of people receiving healing once they realize that they can be healed without prayer through a word of knowledge.

By way of illustration, after about eleven years of ministering healing through words of knowledge, I had an experience in Buenos Aires, Argentina, that changed my life. I began by ministering as I have done for several years, instructing people to stand if the word was for them, and then to raise their hand after they stood if they began to feel something more. My final instruction was to wave both hands once their healing had reached at least 80 percent completion. The people's response in this particular meeting shocked me. I thought they had misunderstood my instructions, because about a quarter of those who stood starting waving both hands over their heads as soon as the word of knowledge was called out.

I instructed the translator to clarify again that the people should not wave their hands if they simply were believing for healing, but only if their healing had manifested by at least 80 percent. Two more times words of knowledge were called out, and each time about a quarter of those who stood began waving both hands.

I told the translator repeatedly, "Clarify my instructions again. I'm sure they do not understand me."

Finally, the translator said to me, "They understand! *You* are the one who does not understand. You have God in a box. Why do you think you have to pray before they are healed? This church was built on the healing gift of Omar Cabrera and his gift of words of knowledge. The people understand words of knowledge and their purpose, and they have faith for healing without needing your prayer." This experience happened in all six cities where I ministered.

This experience changed my ministry forever. Upon returning home to the United States, I told the people in my first meeting what had happened in Argentina. Then I asked, "Do you think God is stronger in Argentina, or do you think our sicknesses are stronger in America?"

Right away the people in that meeting responded, "No!"

I told them, "Then the only thing different is what we are expecting and what the Argentines were expecting. And I believe that God can do here in America what I saw Him do in Argentina."

From that night forward, and now for about the last eighteen years, I have seen people healed by a word of knowledge before anyone even offers one prayer for their healing. This had never happened in my meetings in the 23 years before that experience in Argentina, and it has almost always happened ever since. What changed? It was not the sovereignty of God or the nature of disease that changed, but rather the expectation of the people. Now I am careful to build that expectation through what I say to the people regarding words of knowledge. I am careful to lay a foundation that helps the people understand how words of knowledge can work.

The Intentionality of God

I want to share what I think is the most interesting way of all that faith for healing can increase in a meeting. This way does not focus on what the person in need of healing needs to do, nor on what the minister who is leading needs to do, but rather on what God does. By way of illustration, in March 2013, a young woman came forward at a meeting at Abba's House, a large Southern Baptist church in Hixson, Tennessee. She had had facial reconstruction involving the insertion of three plates, and as a result she had a screw coming loose in her jawbone. She was going to have another surgery to remove the loose screw. But at the meeting she came forward weeping, holding the screw in her hand. God had removed it for her.

While she was still giving her testimony, another man in the congregation started waving his arm wildly. He came forward and testified that he could barely move his right arm due to a break requiring the insertion of seventeen screws between his shoulder and elbow. He now had complete mobility in every way. He demonstrated it by again waving his arm wildly over his head and shoulder. Then he jumped down to the floor and did several push-ups.

There had not yet been any ministry for metal in that meeting. At the point when the young woman had come came forward with the screw in her hand, no one had yet mentioned any ministry taking place to people with surgically implanted materials. Yet I had already determined ahead of time that this was the night I was going to pray for implanted materials. Before I could even do that, God performed these two sovereign healings as an indication of His intentionality. It was a divine set-up that built tremendous faith for healing in that meeting.[6]

Realizing that God was revealing His will and His ways through these two sovereign healings, I spoke it out and it raised the atmosphere of faith in that particular meeting immensely. These two healings of people with implants had occurred without anyone praying for them, and without them even expecting their healing when it happened. Yet through these two initial sovereign healings, God was illustrating His power.

It was wisdom to recognize that what was happening was a "way of God" that He was using as a sign of His intentionality. When I realized the meaning of the healings, it created great faith in me for ministering to others. When I declared it, it also created great faith on the part of people there who were in need of healing, particularly for issues surrounding metal implants in their bodies. At the time, this was the highest percentage of healings for metal in any of my meetings.

Speaking the Amen

Discovering the intentionality of God for a particular meeting through words of knowledge can help explode the faith in the meeting. I have discovered that the gift of words of knowledge, along with the gift of prophecy, is vitally important to creating an atmosphere of faith in the congregation.

Healing breakthrough comes when people understand God's ways. It is important to understand what He is doing through the relationship between the revealed word (in this instance words of knowledge, but in other instances prophetic words), the spoken word and faith.

Whether we are involved in ministering healing to others or in being prayed for ourselves because we need healing, it is important to speak the amen to what God is doing and to recognize how the revelatory gifts can work. These things are key to seeing a healing breakthrough, because they create the prevenient faith of God, solely by grace, when we know His ways.

15

Receiving Revelation

This is the confidence we have in approaching God:
that if we ask anything according to his will, he
hears us. And if we know that he hears us—whatever we ask—we know that we have what we asked
of him.

1 John 5:14–15

I grew up in the Baptist denomination, and the Baptists I knew
were quite the cessationists. Their understanding of a word of
knowledge was very different from how I explain the gift here.
Baptist commentators interpret a word of knowledge as a gift
given to people so that they can understand Scripture and then
communicate doctrine clearly to others.

Because that interpretation deals with human ability and attainment, I don't think it is correct. It is based on someone's ability to be studious, and I find it interesting how many commentators like to go in that direction because it highlights their own
gift—teaching. A word of knowledge deals with information

you cannot learn by studying and cannot attain in any way through human effort. It is revealed to you from heaven.

Words of knowledge help build faith in that they help you know specific things God wants to do in a meeting. If you know something is according to His will, you know that what you ask you will receive. I apply words of knowledge mainly in relationship to healing because healing is my ministry, yet I realize this application of the gift is too limiting. I know a man in another country who has a bachelor's degree in electrical engineering. He holds the highest position in his country in that field, overseeing even people who have a Ph.D. in engineering. How did he rise to such a position in dealing with his country's electrical grid when he has so much less education than others in the same field? It is because when an extremely difficult problem arises and nobody knows how to fix it, the Lord will reveal to him via a word of knowledge what should be done to fix it.

I know of another scientist in one of the greatest universities in the world. A friend of mine is discipling this man, who has won world-famous awards in his field. The Holy Spirit gave this scientist his award-winning formulas via a word of knowledge, but can you imagine the reception if he tried to tell the academic community that? He cannot do so.

I believe God wants to use this gift of words of knowledge to reveal answers to some of the biggest problems facing humanity in our day. Both of these men are examples of God doing just that. God can drop information about anything into your head, which is why I am careful not to limit words of knowledge to the way I usually think of them, in relation to physical healing. A word of knowledge is a revelatory word in which God shows what He wants to do or provides an answer to a problem. It is revelation from Him, nothing you or I figure out on our own. It is information that reveals His will and/or knowledge.

When you get a revelation about the will, intention and timing of God, He uses it to create the next gift, the gift of faith. I am not ready to say that a gift of faith *has* to follow a word of knowledge or is totally based on it. But I am ready to say that a gift of faith often follows a word of knowledge. These two gifts really do work well together.

I remember the first time I ever received a gift of faith. I was 32 years old, and I was doing a healing seminar one night a week for ten weeks in a Presbyterian church. This was a few weeks after Blaine Cook from Vineyard had come to teach at my church, so I had just learned about the gifts from him. And it was my practice to start teaching whatever I learned. During this seminar a woman in her seventies told me she was scheduled to have her carotid arteries reamed out, so to speak. Her arteries were clogging up, and her doctors needed to clear them out to prevent a stroke. Three days before our next meeting, when I was helping my wife put away the dishes, the right carotid artery in my neck started throbbing, literally to the point that I could feel it moving. It was weird. I had never experienced anything like that before, but you could not miss it.

"What's going on?" I said to my wife as I showed her what was happening. "What's this about?"

Then I thought of the woman who told me she had to have her carotid arteries reamed out, so I told DeAnne, "I think I know what this means. God is going to heal that woman of her issues with her carotid arteries."

A few days later, when I was driving to the church, my left carotid artery started throbbing the same way. I told everyone who was riding with me, "I think I know what's going to happen tonight. Wait a minute, I don't *think*—I *know* what God is going to do tonight."

I was confident He was going to ream those arteries out and the woman would not have to have surgery. I was certain it would happen, and I could not wait to get to the meeting. But when I arrived, the woman was not there. I had come a little early and had been watching for her, and now we were twenty minutes into worship and she still had not arrived. I was confused because I was certain that I had understood the word of knowledge and what it meant, and I had faith that God was going to heal her. I was so bothered by the fact that she was not there that I could not even enter into worship. I just walked around saying, *God, I don't understand. What's going on? Why did You do that? She's not even here. I'm so confused.* Then the woman walked in the back door half an hour late.

I ran to her and said, "You're going to get healed tonight! God is going to heal you tonight!" I took her by the hand, walked right up to the front and told the worship team, "Stop! Stop!"

I had never done anything like that in my life. It was the first time I had ever had a word that resulted in a gift of faith.

I said to the crowd, "Watch this! Watch what God is about to do!" I turned around to face the woman and said, "I command those arteries to be reamed out in Jesus' name."

The Spirit of God hit her, and she went backward. She did not fall down, but as she went back you could see the arteries in her neck throbbing. They were going in and out visibly. God performed the surgery; she did not have to have a doctor do it. That was not my faith; it was God's gift of faith.

What if I had told the woman she would be healed and nothing had happened? I believe that would have shown it was not a real gift of faith. This gift of faith is not talking about your faith or mine anymore; it does not involve *our* measure of faith. It is talking about us moving in God's gift of *His* faith given to us. Anytime we are moving by the gift of faith, what we declare must happen because it is not our faith; it is God's faith. The result is not affected by whether or not the person you are praying for has any faith, either. It is about God's faith now.

Look at 1 Corinthians 12:7–10 (emphasis added):

Now to each one the manifestation of the Spirit is given for the common good. To one there is given through the Spirit a message of wisdom, to another a message of knowledge by means of the same Spirit, *to another faith by the same Spirit, to another gifts of healing by that one Spirit, to another miraculous powers*, to another prophecy, to another distinguishing between spirits, to another speaking in different kinds of tongues, and to still another the interpretation of tongues.

Notice that after "to another faith by the same Spirit," the next thing is "to another gifts of healing" (verse 9). Healing is related to faith. As we increase in our faith, we will see more healings. Then it says "to another miraculous powers" (verse 10). These are the working of miracles. I believe that every time a miracle takes place, the operation of the gift of faith preceded the miracle. God can increase our faith through words of knowledge, but there is a difference between the gift of faith and an increase of faith. The gift of faith produces miracles, whereas an increase of faith related to a word of knowledge brings about healings through the gifts of healing.

Just as a side note, let's look more closely for a moment at the gifts of tongues and interpretation that 1 Corinthians 12:10 also mentions. In 1 Corinthians 14:2 (NIV1984) it says, "For anyone who speaks in a tongue does not speak to men but to God." That means the interpretation of tongues should have God as its focus. Tongues are saying things about God; they are addressed to God. They glorify Him and declare His greatness and wonders. In Acts 2, when everyone heard the apostles speaking in tongues in their own languages, they heard the apostles glorifying God and declaring His wonders. Yet most of the interpretations of tongues I have heard in church are directed toward the people, which is really prophecy. I am not saying the interpretation of tongues could not be prophetic in nature, since God is sovereign and can do as He pleases. I am only saying that a more biblical understanding of tongues would be that they are primarily directed toward God, not toward the people. (This was also John Wimber's opinion.)

When you experience God using you in a certain thing and you have seen His faithfulness in that area so many times, it can cause a greater increase in what Paul calls the measure of faith you have. For example, I have a great measure of faith when it comes to praying on a congregational level for people with metal in their body. Sometimes I think it borders on a gift of faith. My friend Bill Johnson has a great measure of faith when it comes to praying for people who have experienced head trauma or who have had accidents that caused serious bone issues. Our measure of faith came through our experiences of seeing healings happen so often in these areas. Now we simply have an expectation that such healings will happen.

Lots of people discover that they have more faith for one thing than for others, based on their history with God. One of my friends has such a measure of faith for the healing of migraine headaches that it borders on a gift of faith. He prays and migraines leave every time. Based on our experiences with healings, we can grow in our measure of faith for certain areas.

I have also seen people come to faith through a prophetic word in which God reveals something about them to someone who does not know them. This supernatural revelation causes them to realize that God is aware of them. For example, Todd White, Jamie Galloway and Will Hart are young men in their thirties who are prophetic evangelists. They have led hundreds of people to the Lord through their gift of prophecy. I once made a video about the type of evangelism they do, known as "power evangelism." In the video you can see how prophetic words affect people, sometimes resulting in their healing and sometimes in their coming to faith. We even talked about making a TV series about power evangelism and calling it *God Squad*. It became a reality through Global Awakening, and today you can find it on YouTube.[1]

We see a biblical example of this kind of evangelism in John 4, which tells the story of Jesus and the woman at the well. She not only comes to faith; she also is used in leading many others to Christ Jesus through her testimony.

> Many of the Samaritans from that town believed in him *because of the woman's testimony*, "He told me everything I ever did." So when the Samaritans came to him, they urged him to stay with them, and he stayed two days. And because of his words many more became believers.
>
> They said to the woman, "We no longer believe just because of what you said; now we have heard for ourselves, and we know that this man really is the Savior of the world."
>
> John 4:39–42, emphasis added

Then there are times when the Holy Spirit quickens God's Word, the Bible, to someone, and through reading it God speaks to that person. I knew a heroin addict who was incarcerated after he hit a police car while he was driving high. In prison he found a booklet that contained some Scriptures. As he read these Scriptures the Holy Spirit brought him under conviction, resulting in his conversion. This is not an uncommon experience. There are many stories of God using the Bible to speak to people as they read it. All of a sudden the Holy Spirit will use the Word to bring conviction or understanding to the searcher, and that person realizes the truth about whatever it is God is saying to him or her.

One example of this is the story of Saint Augustine's conversion, which I told you about in chapter 10. As I mentioned there, Augustine heard a voice telling him repeatedly to read

God's Word: "Take it and read it. Take it and read it." When he opened the Bible, his eyes immediately fell onto Romans 13:13–14, which talks about clothing ourselves with Christ and not satisfying our sinful nature. At this juncture in the Holy Spirit's work, Augustine's great battle involved his desire to live by the flesh and his inability to restrain his sexual desires. Through this passage God spoke to Augustine and showed him the key to practicing continence—clothing himself with the Lord Jesus Christ. Thus the long process of his conversion came to a culmination.[2]

In the next chapter, we will consider in even more detail the relationship of faith to healings and miracles, and we will take a closer look at some of the ways in which God works to build our faith.

16

Faith and the Ways of God

Follow the way of love and eagerly desire spiritual gifts.

1 Corinthians 14:1 NIV1984

When we know the ways of God, it makes us better apostles, prophets, evangelists, pastors and teachers. Yet knowing God's ways is not something only those in the fivefold offices can benefit from; it makes all of us better at leading people to Jesus. It makes us better at building up, comforting and encouraging people. It makes us better disciples. It also makes us better healers, and it contributes to helping us see more people get healed. If we need healing ourselves, knowing God's ways increases our faith.

For example, one teaching says that after you have prayed for people's healing once, you should not pray for them again if you really have faith. If people are in this kind of faith camp, it can cause them to walk out of the presence of God, where healing is taking place, sooner than they should. But if you know the ways of God, you know what to do in those situations.

One time I was praying for a man with a serious physical problem. At first nothing was happening, so we continued to pray for some time. He then started getting hot and his pain got much better, although it was not gone entirely.

Feeling the heat, the man said, "Okay, I believe! I'm ready to leave."

I said, "Do you still feel the heat? Is something still happening?"

He replied, "Yes, I'm still hot."

I told him, "You shouldn't leave yet! This is the Lord's presence for healing. Let's keep praying into this."

He said, "No, it's okay. I believe."

That man did not understand the ways of God. There is a time to believe, and there is a time to receive what you believe. It was that man's time to receive what he was believing for, because it was coming in that place, in that moment. One of the ways God works is through a sick person feeling heat, as that man did. In those moments it is important to stay with the process.

I have been serving God for 45 years and have been praying for the sick for over 35 years, so I want to help you learn these ways of God from my experiences so that you can be healed and/or see more healings in others. A sensation of heat is an indication that God is at work in someone. You should also note that rather than feeling heat, the person being prayed for may sometimes feel electricity or even cold. If you are thinking heat and the person feels cold, that is okay. Whatever form it takes, stay with the healing process.

Another time, we were praying for a little girl who had just had her second liver transplant. Her body had rejected the first one. She was only nine or ten years old, but I believe she had a gift of faith.

This little girl knew I was coming to her church, and she told her pastor, "Take me to the meeting and let him pray for me. I'm going to get healed."

I was looking forward with great excitement to praying for this girl because I sensed that she was full of faith. The Bible talks about *seeing* someone's faith, the way Peter saw the faith of the man at the Gate Beautiful in Acts 3. I knew this was the time—this was the night—for this little girl. But instead of seeing her faith, it was as though I heard her faith in what she told her pastor. As I prayed for her, I interviewed her to find out what was happening.

"I feel cold—ice cold!" she said.

I had never heard that one before. *Well, that's the opposite of hot*, I thought, *so maybe coldness is a sign of demons involved here or something.*

The girl had a tube in place where there was an infection in her body because she was already rejecting the second liver transplant. If the rejection continued, we all knew she would die. She would not undergo a third transplant. The infection coming out of that tube was causing a fever, which fights infection. But when we prayed, she felt ice cold, and in that process she got healed. Her body did not reject the liver, and the coldness did not signify a demon. It was the presence of God on that girl, working in a way opposite of what we might expect. Sometimes you have to realize that God is doing something new—or at least new to you.

Not Some Silly Manifestation

Have you enjoyed the privilege of having God use you to bring someone into the Kingdom? Isn't it exciting to partner with God and become a co-laborer with Him because you have gained an understanding of His ways pertaining to salvation and the work of the Spirit? What a great privilege that we are joint heirs and co-laborers with Christ.

Are you familiar with the ways of God in those moments? For example, when we see people tear up as they hear the Gospel, we recognize that their tears are a manifestation of the Spirit. It is a sign that He is working in them. We need to realize the importance of giving value to this manifestation. There also are different manifestations related to other actions of the Holy Spirit. We need to be aware that these are not just some silly little manifestations. They are evidence of the presence of God with us and on the person whom we are praying for in that moment. Such manifestations might come as peace, perspiration, goose bumps, blotching of the skin around the neck and/or chest, trembling in the body, heat or energy that feels like low-voltage electricity. Sometimes these manifestations are present all over the body, and other times they manifest only in the part of the body where healing needs to occur.

When we are praying as a vessel of God and a manifestation begins to happen, it is one of the most intimate, personal times we can experience with God. We should cherish those moments. The God of the universe is right there with us, touching a person and responding to our prayers. This is precious; this is gold. We should not ignore or easily dismiss such moments and manifestations.

Sometimes when you are praying for people, rather than feeling heat, cold or energy they will feel peace. They will feel the Prince of Peace manifesting His peace on them. Peace is not some second-class manifestation either. Peace is right up there with the rest of the indications that God is present and at work. Remember that the ways of God are both precious and diverse.[1]

Sometimes people do not feel anything when you pray. Sometimes when you get done praying, there is no manifestation at all and the people don't seem any better. But then you find out a few days later that they were healed.

Once when I visited a church where one of my close friends was pastoring, I prayed for a man in a wheelchair. He had contracted AIDS through a blood transfusion and had ended up in hospice. At the point when I met him, he had been given only a few weeks to live. I prayed several times for him, and none of the manifestations we have been talking about occurred. I have had this happen enough times that I know better than to base whether or not I think someone got healed on the manifestations alone. But in this guy's case, I really did not think anything had happened to him. When I went back to that church eight or ten months later, however, this big guy came up to talk to me. He was not tall, but he was built.

"Do you recognize me?" the guy asked.

"No, I really don't," I replied.

"Do you remember a man in a wheelchair who wore a patch over one eye?"

"Yes. The guy was seeing double out of one eye, and he was close to dying of AIDS," I said. "What happened to him?"

"That's me!" he cried. "I am that man! I didn't feel any better the day you prayed, or the next day, or the day after that. But on the third morning I woke up feeling stronger. Soon I was totally healed."

That man at death's door got healed without any visible manifestations at all. We need to be careful not to put so much emphasis on God's presence being tied to certain manifestations that if they don't happen, we don't believe He is healing and don't believe anything is happening while we pray.

Another way of God I want to mention is that sometimes people do not feel any manifestations, yet they still are aware that something is happening. They might not feel heat, cold, electric energy or peace, but what stands out to them is something different that they are *not* feeling. What they are aware of is that they are *not* feeling as much pain. And that is making all the difference for them. When that happens, thank God for it and bless what He is doing.

Celebrating God's Presence

Learning the ways of God is important so that when you are praying for the sick (or you are the one being prayed for), you begin to see and experience how He is working and you are able to recognize what He is doing. Seeing God work to heal people brings the same excitement as you get when you share the Gospel and people start crying. It gives you a sense that God is doing something here. And it is not so that you or I can get worked up and brag about how many people we have seen healed through our ministry. It is not a competition to see which of us had the most people healed when we prayed for them. It is about God going with us and working His ways through us to bring a healing breakthrough in people's lives.

What if we are going through our Christian life never seeing the kind of manifestations I am talking about? Could it be that God is not with us? I certainly don't want to go to a church where He is not with us. On the other hand, I also don't want to go where people believe in manifestations as a doctrine. As I said, sometimes manifestations don't happen even though a healing is taking place. Yet where there is no experience of God's tangible presence in our midst, I have to wonder if we really know and understand His ways. I also think it is so important that we all understand His ways—both those of us who are ministering healing and those of us who are being ministered to. In fact, understanding God's ways is important to teaching, evangelism, prophecy and healing.

There is such priceless value to having the God of the universe working in and through us. When it happens, we should be like kids at Christmas who just got the best gift underneath the Christmas tree. We should be excited, joyous and celebrative. I cherish every manifestation that points to the reality that the presence of almighty God is right here, working with us.

One time several years ago, I went through a period when the level of anointing, presence and healings diminished for me. It grieved and saddened me, so I began to pray, *God, if I have done anything wrong, show me. If I have grieved You in any way, show me. I don't want to live life void of Your presence. The moments when You come are the most exciting moments of my life. You can do anything You want to me; just don't leave me alone! I don't want to live my Christian life without Your presence!*

It was not long before that season ended with a sense of God's presence touching me in a greater way. God's presence is a gift. As a parent, I love giving things to my children. My giving is unconditional; it is not based on how well they perform. When they get excited about me giving them something, however, and when they are grateful and thankful, it opens up a desire in me to bless them even more. I want to do even more for them. I think the same is true of our heavenly Father. As God sees how much we celebrate His works and how thankful we are for them, He wants to do even more in and through us.

A Migrating Manifestation

Sometimes when you pray for people, the manifestation that occurs is that their pain gets worse and even migrates around in their body. This is not one of the ways of God, but something quite the opposite. When I first started praying for the sick I did not understand this, and it caught me off guard. I went to the hospital and started praying for this young woman who was experiencing intense pain.

"How are you?" I asked after the prayer.

"I'm worse!" she replied. "My pain got worse when you prayed for me!"

If you don't understand this manifestation, you may have a tendency to think, *Lord, I knew I didn't have any faith. I knew I wasn't anointed. I prayed and this person got worse!* But the problem is not in you at all. If you begin to pray and almost instantly someone's pain gets worse or moves around, you should recognize that there is another explanation. The presence of Jesus you brought in with you is actually aggravating an afflicting spirit that is troubling the person. (Note, however, that I am not saying this is always the case when a terminally ill person does not get healed. When you pray for someone who is dying and he or she gets worse and dies, it is not necessarily demonic. He or she just didn't get healed.)

I remember the first time I prayed for someone and the pain started moving around from place to place. I was praying for a Catholic lady at a home group. She never was able to sleep well, so she was tired all the time. She suffered great pain in her left shoulder, and every night after a few hours of sleep, her shoulder pain would get so intense that it would wake her up. We began to pray for her, and then I interviewed her to see what was happening.

"My shoulder pain is gone," she told me.

"Thank You, Jesus!" I began to say. "Hallelujah!" I was so excited for her.

"Wait a minute," she interrupted me. "The pain is awful in my neck now."

I had never experienced pain migrating in someone before, but I began to pray for her neck, which seemed like the next obvious step. Then I interviewed her again.

"The pain is getting better," she told me. "Wait—now it's gone!"

"Thank You, Jesus!" I said again. "Hallelujah!"

"Oh, wait a minute, now the pain is in my right shoulder instead of my left one."

At first I could not figure it out, but I knew this was not a normal kind of pain. Then I realized it did not have a natural cause at all. The cause of her pain was an afflicting spirit. At that point I switched my prayer of petition to one of command.

"In Jesus' name, I command this spirit of affliction to *leave*," I said.

The pain went into her elbow next.

"I command this spirit to *leave*. Get out of here in Jesus' name!" I commanded again.

The pain went into her wrist, so I commanded the spirit to leave a third time, and this time it left. For sixteen years after that, she never had that type of shoulder pain again and was able to sleep without being awakened by pain.

On another occasion when I was in India, we were doing a crusade in a really poor city. A Hindu man was carried to the meeting on his friend's back because the bottoms of his feet hurt so badly that he could not walk. We started to pray for him, and he started getting better.

"My feet don't hurt!" he exclaimed.

"Thank You, Jesus!" I responded.

But then he added, "The pain is in my knees now."

We prayed again, and the pain left his knees.

"Now the pain is in my hips," he said.

This time I knew that a spirit of affliction was causing the migrating pain, so we prayed again and I commanded it to leave. It went, all right—back into his knees. We prayed and commanded it again, and it went into his foot. We prayed and commanded it again, and it left. He was healed, and I led him to Jesus. Then he walked home himself, without needing his friend to carry him.

Faith and the Excellent Way

When it comes to how the gifts work, understanding the ways of God can increase our measure of faith. It is a matter of cause and effect. The revelatory gifts reveal what God wants to do. When we learn the ways of God, we then can understand the meaning and purpose of a revelatory gift when it manifests. A gift of revelation creates stronger faith. But this is done by the grace of God manifested by the gift of revelation, which is itself a manifestation of grace. Grace is a divine empowerment, so any of the gifts are manifestations of God's grace.

In fact, the gifts are often referred to as "gracelets." The gracelet of faith is created by the gracelet of revelation, and the gracelet of faith releases the gracelet of healing. There is a causal relationship between revelation, faith, and healing and miracles.

The kind of faith that releases the gracelet of healing does not come from working ourselves up emotionally. It does not come if we just pray in tongues hard enough, or if we just say "I believe, I believe, I believe" often enough. I am not talking about manufacturing a greater degree of faith for ourselves. Instead of revving ourselves up, we dial down into that place of peace where we are listening with an understanding of the ways of God. Our understanding of His ways pertaining to the charismata (gifts) causes us to have confidence in Him. We then have faith to speak to the condition we want to see changed.

When Paul discusses the gifts in 1 Corinthians 12, he talks about having faith "by the same Spirit" (verse 9). That is important because it is not faith that you or I manufacture; it comes *by the Spirit*. (We talked about that a little in the previous chapter.)

Here is another thing I find interesting. In the last part of the last verse of chapter 12, Paul says, "And now I will show you the most excellent way," and then he moves into chapter 13, widely known as the love chapter. Yet right before that he says, "But eagerly desire the greater gifts" (1 Corinthians 12:31 NIV1984). And if you skip ahead to the first verse of chapter 14, he says, "Follow the way of love and eagerly desire spiritual gifts, especially the gift of prophecy" (NIV1984).

Do you see a pattern? Even though Paul is about to address "the most excellent way" of love in chapter 13, he still emphasizes both before and after how very important it is to desire the spiritual gifts. Any interpretation that says chapter 13 presents a better way than the gifts is wrong. Paul is not saying that what we need is love, not the gifts. He is saying that we need the gifts and we need to desire them, but in the midst of that we need to learn how to exercise them with love as our motivation.

Faith *in* God or Faith *of* God?

In the first few verses of 1 Corinthians 13, Paul goes back and talks about the different gifts. He talks about tongues, he talks about prophecy, he talks about wisdom, he talks about knowledge and he talks about faith—the gifts he just enumerated in chapter 12. But look what he says about faith: "And if I have a faith that can move mountains, but do not have love, I am nothing" (verse 2).

We have to remember that Paul is not talking about a general understanding of faith here; he is talking about the gift of faith that comes by the Spirit, as he said in chapter 12. Now look at Mark 11:22–24:

> "Have faith in God," Jesus answered. "Truly I tell you, if anyone says to this mountain, 'Go, throw yourself into the sea,' and does not doubt in their heart but believes that what they say will happen, it will be done for them. Therefore I tell you, whatever you ask for in prayer, believe that you have received it, and it will be yours."

Just as with the New International Version that I am quoting, in most translations the beginning of this passage says, "Have faith *in* God." In the Greek, however, this could just as easily be translated, "Have faith *of* God." There is a huge difference in how we apply those two translations. Having faith *in* God puts the burden on me to come to a place of having such strong faith in Him. It involves my faith, my ability to believe in God. Having the faith *of* God really is different. This kind of faith comes as a gift that God gives us. He supplies this kind of faith by the Spirit. It goes beyond our faith that we can have in God; it is God's faith given to us.

Six versions of the Bible actually do translate the phrase we are looking at as "Have faith *of* God" or "Have faith *from* God."[2] If it could be translated correctly in either of those ways, *of* or *from*, then why has it so often been translated using the word *in* instead, "Have faith *in* God"? I think the reason was because most Bible translators were scholarly people who had studied Greek and Hebrew. They were part of what we call academia, or higher education. I do not know of any translators who also were healing evangelists. So when they were faced with the options "Have faith *in* God" or "Have faith *of* [or *from*] God," they probably figured, *I don't understand what "Have faith of* [or *from*] *God" would mean, so "Have faith in God" would make more sense.*

If you had never experienced the gift of God's faith, you would translate the passage in a way that made more sense to you instead. But I believe this phrase should be translated as "have faith *of* God," and I will tell you why. There is only one other place, not counting the parallel in Matthew 21:21 to our Mark 11 passage, where the Bible makes reference to a faith that can move mountains. This is in 1 Corinthians 13:2, where Paul says, "If I have the gift of prophecy and can fathom all mysteries and all knowledge, and if I have a faith that can move mountains, but do not have love, I am nothing."

The reason this is so important is that it is clear from Paul's reference to "a faith that can move mountains" that he is referring to the gift of faith he mentions in 1 Corinthians 12:9, "to another [is given] faith by the same Spirit." The faith that can move a mountain is not a natural faith; it is a gift of faith provided by the Holy Spirit. This fits well with translating Mark 11:22 as "Have faith *of* God," which is another way of saying, as Paul did, "faith by the same Spirit." This brings about unity and total agreement in Scripture regarding the kind of faith that can move a mountain.

The phrase "move a mountain" is a Jewish euphemism for enabling people to overcome great problems or obstacles in their lives. I believe this goes beyond natural ability, requiring the supernatural power of God that is released through the gift of faith—the faith *of* God or the faith *from* God.

Dr. Charles Price, a healing evangelist from the 1920s to the 1940s, wrote a book called *The Real Faith*. A lawyer trained at Oxford University, he became an extremely liberal Methodist pastor and did not believe in the supernatural. Then he got healed at an Aimee Semple McPherson meeting and changed his beliefs about healing. After that, great miracles occurred in his ministry. In the original version of his book (not the adapted and edited one), he emphasized what I have been teaching. In chapter 18 ahead, I will share more of what he says about faith, because his explanations are some of the best I have ever seen. But I want to highlight here his understanding of the type of faith that creates miracles. He said that it comes as a gift in the moment, and he added that it is not something we have to strive for or generate. In fact, we cannot work up enough of that kind of faith. Instead, we pray the prayer, "Lord, give me Your faith."[3]

I believe that God wants to release this gift of faith, but if we don't understand how He creates it, and if we don't understand His ways, we don't accept the gift because "my people are destroyed from lack of knowledge" (Hosea 4:6). This takes us back again to the question, What are the ways of God? It is important that we understand them in relation to faith.

No More Playing It Safe

As I gained an understanding of the ways of God, my faith increased to the point that I would declare things I never would have dared to before. I never had faith to pray for people with metal in their bodies until I heard that God was using a man for that, James Maloney. I had both James Maloney and Bill Johnson come to speak for me at a conference in England, and I asked James to lay hands on Bill and me for a transference of the anointing for healing of people with metal in their bodies.

"We want to experience what you're experiencing," I told James. "We want to begin to see people with problems from metal in their bodies being healed."

James prayed for us, yet I still did not pray for anybody with metal for months after that. Not until Bill came and told me later, "I've started seeing people get healed of metal. They're able to do things they shouldn't be able to do. I don't know if the metal is disappearing or bending."

That gave me faith to try. The first time I prayed such prayers for the healing of metal issues, nothing happened. I had expected something to happen. I had what I thought was faith for it to happen. I also declared that it would happen. Yet not one person was healed of metal complications in his or her body. I was so shocked that nobody was healed that I determined it would be a long time before I had enough faith to try to pray for people with complications from metal again. I thought it would take months, if not years, before I would have enough faith to pray for metal again.

Then God set me up in the next meeting. In all the thousands of meetings I have done, I had never had anyone bring in an X-ray that showed the metal in his or her body. God set that up, however, when a man in Colorado handed me a copy of his X-ray. It showed 23 screws and 4 metal rods in his neck. He told me he was in excruciating pain. He had a morphine pump to help him cope with his pain levels.

I recognized this unusual occurrence as one of the ways of God that He uses to create faith. The copy of the man's X-ray that I held gave me faith to pray for healing of metal in that meeting. The man was healed, along with 23 of the 47 people who stood up because they had issues with metal that had been surgically implanted in their bodies.

From this meeting forward, the healing of people with metal in their bodies started happening over and over. Now I have a gift of faith for healing people who have metal in their bodies. This is the only condition for which I have a gift of faith in every service. I can trace the gift back to the timing and experience of receiving that X-ray from the man with screws and rods in his neck. But my gift continued and developed from seeing people get healed every time I talk about healing of metal. I believe it is now based on my numerous experiences seeing the faithfulness of God in healing these conditions.

When I went to Argentina, something else happened. I saw people getting healed by a word of knowledge *before* I even prayed. I had never seen that happen in America, but when I returned to the States I had faith that it could happen. I even had enough faith to say in a meeting, "This is what I think *is* going to happen. Though I have never seen it happen here in America, you're going to get healed before we pray."

I don't think it was a gift of faith that time, but I had a greater measure of faith based on my previous experience. Then I began to see Bill Johnson doing something different that increased my faith. People would stand up in meetings in response to Bill giving words of knowledge. He did not pray for them; he just said things like, "If you have a tailbone problem, sit down really hard three times and you'll be healed."

When I heard him saying that kind of thing, I thought, *Oh! My! Gosh! Bill is passing me up.* And he did. I went to several meetings and watched him do things like that.

Then he came to me and said, "Randy, you're playing it too safe. You're so close. You just need to give some words and have people stand up. Then whatever comes into your head, say it."

So I went to a southern state and I got a word like that. I felt it—a tailbone problem. Bill had said to sit down three times, so I asked, *Lord, what do we do here?*

Seven, I heard.

I said to the people with tailbone issues, "Sit down really hard seven times, and I believe you'll be healed."

There were several people, and they all sat down hard seven times.

"Check it out; you should be healed. Now, don't be nice; be truthful. Are you at least 80 percent better?"

All of them said they were, except one man.

"Well, how are you?" I asked him.

"No different," he answered.

So I said, "Do it again seven times, really hard."

He did, and I said, "Check it out again. How are you now?"

"It's gone," he replied. "All the pain is gone!"

That night, I did the same kind of thing many times for many different words of knowledge, and I was so happy with the results. I was so excited about everything that I decided to take a video of the healings to my school and show it to the students.

"Look! I said . . . because it's what came into my head," I told them. "And then I said . . . because that's what came. And look what God did!"

Leveling Up in Faith

Through practice and through seeing God's faithfulness, my measure of faith has grown much bigger over the years. Now I really am confident about what God will do. When it comes to healing and miracles, you are at a certain level in your walk with God. But He can level you up, so to speak. Words of knowledge can increase your faith for certain things God wants to do in a particular meeting. And if you understand the connection between words of knowledge, increased faith and the release of power, then you are making the right connections. You are beginning to understand how faith comes from understanding the ways of God, and how faith is in itself a divine enablement or a grace to believe. When you make these connections, you will see a greater breakthrough in healing.

Then there is the measure of faith. It can grow through your experience of God and His faithfulness to you in certain areas. As a person who is praying for others experiences healings in a particular area, faith for that area increases. As time goes on and more healings occur, the person who is ministering develops a stronger faith as a result of seeing God heal with such regularity. Faith has been given or created in the person to see that particular type of healing.

For example, I told you that I have faith to pray for people with chronic pain or loss of mobility due to surgeries,[4] and I almost always pray at least once in every series of meetings for those with surgically implanted material in their bodies. Due to the frequency of healings I have seen in these areas, I have great faith for people with these issues to be healed. God has leveled me up in my faith for those areas. So have *faith in God* and pray for the *faith of God*. May your measure of faith increase with the gifts.

17

Different Types of Faith

For by the grace given me I say to every one of you: Do not think of yourself more highly than you ought, but rather think of yourself with sober judgment, in accordance with the faith God has distributed to each of you. For just as each of us has one body with many members, and these members do not all have the same function, so in Christ we, though many, form one body, and each member belongs to all the others. We have different gifts, according to the grace given to each of us.

Romans 12:3–6

Dr. Herbert Benson, the professor of medicine at Harvard Medical School whom I quoted in chapter 11, believes that God has wired us for Himself, and that we are wired in such a way as to find faith enormously healing.[1]

I agree with Dr. Benson. God has hardwired us for Himself and for faith. I believe faith can and does produce healing in our bodies. Dr. Benson would concur. Nevertheless, unlike him,

I believe that faith must acknowledge a divine power that goes beyond a posited materialistic, naturalistic chain of causality. Faith is key to healing and miracles. Actually, it is at the heart of both. Furthermore, I believe the type of faith needed for greater kinds of healing and miracles is not human faith, mind-body-spirit interconnectedness or a placebo effect at work. That type of faith is a gift from God, an infusion of the faith *of* God.[2]

Miracles that are greater than healings are dependent on the faith *of* God, but significant healings are dependent on our measure of faith *in* God and in the Gospel of the Kingdom. I also believe healing can happen through a naturalistic faith that is not dependent on an understanding of the Gospel or the use of our authority in the name of Jesus. Here I am referring to the same type of faith that Dr. Benson refers to, where it is a naturalistic ability—the kind of faith that we call in popular language "mind over matter." Like Dr. Leslie Weatherhead, however, who wrote *Psychology, Religion, and Healing* (Abingdon Press, 1952) and *Wounded Spirits* (Abingdon Press, 1962), I agree that this kind of faith is *not* the same as the faith that God supplies supernaturally. The results of naturalistic faith are much less pronounced than the results produced by faith in the Gospel and by using our authority in Jesus' name.

It is not that faith itself is the agency of the healing. Rather, faith is the connection between the true agency—the energy of God—and the area that needs healing. In this sense, at least, it is partially true that we are healed by our faith, because faith is the means by which we experience the power of God in the form of His energy for healing. The power and energy of God are what heals a person, with faith as the means by which we experience them. We must also remember that mountain-moving faith is a grace gift, a "gracelet," not a human attainment.

In one of my doctoral thesis conclusions, I assert that people's theology has a tremendous effect on their faith. I based this conclusion on the study in which I ministered to thousands of people on five different continents and interviewed hundreds of them. Our experience also has a tremendous effect on our faith, as does knowing someone who has been healed of something in a particular area. Sometimes being aware of another person's healing in a certain area results in our own healing.

As I talked about earlier, learning the "ways of God" is vitally important when it comes to creating an atmosphere of faith in a congregation for healing breakthrough. As a side note, I want to mention that knowing the "ways of God" is a reference to Moses' words in Exodus 33:13: "If you are pleased with me, teach me your ways so I may know you and continue to find favor with you. Remember that this nation is your people." Actually, the entire chapter of Exodus 33 is significant. In verse 18, Moses moves from asking God to teach him His ways to asking God to show him His glory: "Then Moses said, 'Now show me your glory.'" What can we learn from this dialogue between Moses and God? First, learning the ways of God is dependent on the presence of God, not reducing our relationship with Him to principles or precepts. Second, Moses understood that learning the ways of God was key in knowing God and finding favor with Him. Third, Moses not only wanted to know God's ways, know Him better and find favor; he also wanted to see God's glory. Fourth, from a study of God's glory (though not in this particular passage) we learn that the primary way God revealed His glory in the Bible was through signs and wonders, healings and miracles.

This connection between learning the ways of God and seeing the glory of God is very strong. Without learning the ways of God, you will find it difficult to co-labor with Him and His glory. Without learning the ways of God, you will miss His leadings. Without learning the ways of God, you will not experience the same level of faith that comes from knowing His will in a particular situation. And without knowing His will, you will not have greater faith that He will respond to your prayers of command. When you know that what you are commanding is His will, then you do have that faith, as revealed through His revelatory gifts. As 1 John 5:14–15 says, "This is the confidence we have in approaching God: that if we ask anything according to his will, he hears us. And if we know that he hears us—whatever we ask—we know that we have what we asked of him."

In addition to knowing God's ways, I believe a number of other things are important to creating an atmosphere of faith. Among them are using live healing testimonies, sharing videos of such testimonies and sharing solid biblical teaching regarding healing. Moreover, I believe that although the research for my thesis created a confound in regard to words of knowledge, such words also are important in creating greater faith for healing and miracles. I have seen a strong connection between words of knowledge and healing and miracles.

Much mystery remains in regard to healing, and many questions remain unanswered. Yet if we wait until all the questions are answered before we pray for healing (or before we are prayed for so we can be healed), healing ministry would never take place. Some of the answers are hidden in the unknown contingencies of the human context, including the power of the mind. Some of the answers are hidden in the mystery of faith itself—the faith of the individual, corporate faith and the gift of faith. Some of the answers are hidden in the sovereign purposes of God.

Though much more remains for us to understand, I am growing in my understanding of the ways of God pertaining to healing. Some of these ways concern faith. Some concern the relationship between our declarations and faith. Some concern the relationship between healing and divine revelations that come through the gifts of the Holy Spirit—especially words of knowledge, prophecy, faith, gifts of healings and miraculous powers. I hope that whether you are praying for others or are in need of healing yourself, you are growing in your understanding, too, as we look together at the different aspects of creating an atmosphere of faith conducive to a healing breakthrough.

Rhema, Logos and Faith

In his article on faith *(pistis)* in the *Theological Dictionary of the New Testament*, Rudolf Bultmann gives us a limited understanding of faith. He notes that faith has multiple meanings, including dependence upon, trust in, obedience to, expectation of and certainty of the Triune God.[3] I believe it is necessary, however, that we are careful not to rely solely on word studies to find information about the relationship of faith to miracles. I believe we must look beyond word studies to learn more about the nature of faith and its place in fulfilling the Gospel of the Kingdom. (I am not referring to the faith of coming to Christ here, but the meaning of faith once a person has come to Christ.) Two good sources for this kind of research are the works of Jon Ruthven and Gary Greig.[4]

The New Covenant was meant to enable God's followers to hear directly from Him via the Holy Spirit. This hearing would produce faith, and that faith would result in the mighty works of God.[5] Sometimes, however, a problem arises not so much in the ability of Christians to hear, as in their ability to recognize that what they are hearing (through various means of perception) is from God.[6] In light of the importance of both hearing and perceiving, let's consider the importance of the *rhema* and *logos* of God.

The words *rhema* and *logos* have the meaning of communication, as in a word spoken from someone to someone else.[7]

Although much has been made of a distinction between the two words in charismatic circles, there is not good support for this differentiation.[8] *Logos* often refers to the expression of a thought, as in a message or a discourse, whereas *rhema* often refers to that which is said or spoken, as in an utterance. Though the meanings of these two words overlap in the Greek New Testament, one can contrast them in this way: *Logos* is the message itself; *rhema* is the communication of that message.[9]

Regardless of whether *logos* or *rhema* is used to describe divine revelation in the New Testament, the connection is very strong between faith and hearing and receiving revelation from God. A word from God allows us to know the specific will of God in a specific situation, thereby causing great faith in us that He will answer our prayer for a healing or miracle.

Such revelatory words are often called prophecy or words of knowledge in charismatic, Pentecostal and Third Wave[10] churches. The more traditional Reformed churches are much more unlikely to use such terms, preferring instead to speak of "inspiration from God." In the Baptist church my grandmother attended, people's descriptions for such communications was "the Lord told me" or "the Lord led me." These revelatory gifts happen more often to people who expect them. Often called "words from God," they are unmerited gifts that come to those who understand how to recognize such words and pay attention for them.

Revelation and Relationship

These revelatory gifts often come to those who have a good relationship with God, as Jesus pointed out in His Upper Room discourse. Let's look at some of the things He says about that.

If you love me, you will obey what I command. And I will ask the Father, and he will give you another Counselor to be with you forever—the Spirit of truth. The world cannot accept him, because it neither sees him nor knows him. But you know him, for he lives with you and will be in you. I will not leave you as orphans; I will come to you. Before long, the world will not see me anymore, but you will see me. Because I live, you also will live. On that day you will realize that I am in my Father, and you are in me, and I am in you. Whoever has my commands and obeys them, he is the one who loves me. He who loves me will be loved by my Father, and I too will love him and *show myself to him.*

John 14:15–21 NIV1984 (emphasis added)

I am the true vine, and my Father is the gardener. He cuts off every branch in me that bears no fruit, while every branch that does bear fruit he prunes so that it will be even more fruitful. You are already clean because of the word I have spoken to you. Remain in me, and I will remain in you. No branch can bear fruit by itself; it must remain in the vine. Neither can you bear fruit unless you remain in me. I am the vine; you are the branches. If a man remains in me and I in him, he will bear much fruit; apart from me you can do nothing. If anyone does not remain in me, he is like a branch that is thrown away and withers; such branches are picked up, thrown into the fire and burned. If you remain in me and my words remain in you, ask whatever you wish, and it will be given you. This is to my Father's glory, that you bear much fruit, showing yourselves to be my disciples.

John 15:1–8 NIV1984

I have much more to say to you, more than you can now bear. But when he, the Spirit of truth, comes, he will guide you into all truth. *He will not speak on his own; he will speak only what he hears, and he will tell you what is yet to come. He will bring glory to me by taking from what is mine and making it known to you.* All that belongs to the Father is mine. That is why I said the Spirit will take from what is mine and *make it known to you.*

John 16:12–15 NIV1984 (emphasis added)

As we can see from what Jesus said in these passages, revelation and relationship are closely intertwined. The revelatory gifts flow out of our relationship with God.

Degrees of Faith

Scripture uses the word *faith* in multiple ways. In some instances, faith is used similarly to how we use it today, to mark something one may believe. In other instances it delves deeper, entering into the realm of healing and miracles. Scripture explores both having the faith to see healing and miracles and experiencing them for oneself. It also uses the word *faith* as it relates to salvation, sanctification and righteousness.

In addition to the different meanings of the word *faith*, one might also say there are degrees of faith. Jesus seemed to indicate this. He compared the centurion's great faith to that of all Israel when He marveled at the man's words and said, "Assuredly, I say to you, I have not found such great faith, not even in Israel!" (Matthew 8:10). Jesus also made a statement about the small size of the disciples' faith:

Jesus rebuked the demon, and it came out of the boy, and he was healed from that moment. Then the disciples came to Jesus in private and asked, "Why couldn't we drive it out?" He replied, "Because you have so little faith. I tell you the truth, if you have faith as small as a mustard seed, you can say to this mountain, 'Move from here to there' and it will move."

Matthew 17:18–20 NIV1984

In fact, Jesus referred to different degrees of faith both large and small numerous times in the gospels. To name a few instances, Jesus referred to having little faith throughout the gospel of Matthew, in Matthew 6:30; 8:26; 14:31; 16:8; and 17:20. He also referred to little faith in Luke 12:28. He referred to having great faith in Matthew 8:10; 15:28; Luke 7:9; and John 14:12.

God-Infused Faith

All faith is not the same, at least in relation to its cause. Sometimes our past experiences of healing cause faith to arise. Sometimes our confident expectation based on God's promises causes faith. We must make a distinction, however, between those causes of faith and the gift of faith itself. One is caused by former experience or by meditating on biblical promises, and the other is a divine gift of grace.

As I have mentioned already, the God-infused faith that is a gift is closely related to miracles (though also to healing). I have seen scores of thousands of healings so far, but probably fewer than one hundred miracles. In every miracle, it seemed a gift of faith was present—the mountain-moving faith Jesus referred to that comes as a gift. With it, there comes a certainty within us that God is about to heal or perform a miracle.

God's faith comes from God's grace, and this grace is dependent on our relationship with Jesus and our abiding in Him. As Dr. Jim McClure points out in his book *Grace Revisited*, divine enablement is one of the concepts of grace. He writes,

When the word grace is used in the New Testament, there is the suggestion of God's presence. Therefore grace could be defined as "God's empowering presence," and as such it includes all that is meant by the word "power," that is, both divine authority and dynamic power.[11]

This faith for miracles and even for healing is not constant. It is not constituted; it is situational, as John Wimber so powerfully taught. In other words, it is not a gift someone would move in regularly, and it is not a gift someone would be noted for having. Rather, it occurs infrequently and situationally, and God infuses it into us.

We see the relationship between grace, gifts and faith in Romans 12:3–6, where Paul speaks of a measure of faith:

> For by the grace given me I say to every one of you: Do not think of yourself more highly than you ought, but rather think of yourself with sober judgment, in accordance with the measure of faith God has given you. . . . We have different gifts, according to the grace given us. If a man's gift is prophesying, let him use it in proportion to his faith.

Verse 6 speaks of gifts according to the grace given us, and then relates the operation of the gift of grace, or a "gracelet," to faith. This raises some questions for us. If gifts are based in and on the grace of God and are divine enablements, and if gifts operate by faith, and if faith itself is seen as rooted in grace or as a manifestation of grace, doesn't this seem to make the operation of the gifts to be of grace? If this is so, then are there ways that God infuses this grace, and if so, how does this happen? I cover this topic more fully in chapter 5 of my doctoral thesis, which addresses the questions of faith's relationship to the gifts of the Holy Spirit, and whether or not there are ways to bring about a higher probability of receiving a healing or miracle.[12]

Saving Faith

The Bible not only speaks of faith that produces healing and miracles; it also speaks of faith for salvation. I am not trying to differentiate between the quality of these different types of faith, and I am not saying that one is less supernatural than the other. I simply want to point out that the purpose or object of each type of faith is different.

One type of faith relates to God working outside a person's salvation. Most of the time this type of faith is related to physical situations like healing and miracles, or to spiritual realities, like deliverance from demons. The other type of faith relates to an individual's salvation and/or sanctification and righteousness. Let's look at some Scriptures that refer to that latter type of faith.[13]

Therefore, since we have been justified through faith, we have peace with God through our Lord Jesus Christ, through whom we have gained access by faith into this grace in which we now stand. And we rejoice in the hope of the glory of God.

Romans 5:1–2 NIV1984

But righteousness that is by faith says: "Do not say in your heart, 'Who will ascend into heaven?'" (that is, to bring Christ down) . . . But what does it say? "The word is near you; it is in your mouth and in your heart," that is, the word of faith we are proclaiming.

Romans 10:6–8 NIV1984

Consequently, faith comes from hearing the message, and the message is heard through the word of Christ.[14]

Romans 10:17 NIV1984

Consider this: You do not support the root, but the root supports you. You will say then, "Branches were broken off so that I could be grafted in." Granted. But they were broken off because of unbelief, and you stand by faith. Do not be arrogant, but be afraid.

Romans 11:18–20 NIV1984

For by the grace given to me I say to every one of you: Do not think of yourself more highly than you ought, but rather think of yourself with sober judgment, in accordance with the measure of faith God has given you. . . . We have different gifts, according to the grace given us. If a man's gift is prophesying, let him use it in proportion to his faith.[15]

Romans 12:3, 6 NIV1984

My message and my preaching were not with wise and persuasive words, but with a demonstration of the Spirit's power, so that your faith might not rest on men's wisdom, but on God's power.

1 Corinthians 2:4 NIV1984

The faith these Scriptures refer to is the type that deals with salvation, not miracles.

It is my hope that the contents of this chapter have opened up to you a new understanding of the subject of faith and have shown you how faith is so closely related to grace—especially to the revelational gifts of the Holy Spirit (words of knowledge and prophecy). From our examination of Scripture, we have seen that one's *faith* can mean many things. It can mean the faith to believe, the faith to see and experience healings and miracles or the faith of the righteous and sanctified. Part of understanding the "ways of God" involves being able to identify the types of faith that Scripture refers to, and also knowing how faith arises and how it operates. It is an atmosphere of faith, after all, that can usher in a healing breakthrough.

18

The Probability of Healing

Now faith is confidence in what we hope for and
assurance about what we do not see.

Hebrews 11:1

I recently finished my doctoral degree program at United Theological Seminary, a United Methodist seminary in Dayton, Ohio. I mentioned earlier that for my thesis research, I conducted a study that included researching the effectiveness of six independent variables in increasing the probability of someone receiving healing. My thesis focused on healings specifically associated with people who have surgically implanted materials in their bodies. The healings had to be marked by at least an 80 percent reduction in pain or chronic pain, or an 80 percent improvement in range of motion.

In my study, I not only proved that healing was taking place in my meetings; I also attempted to find out which variables increased the probability of healing. I chose to study the following six independent variables related to faith to see if they increased the percentage of people being healed:

1. The theology of the people involved—both the person in need of healing and the person praying for that healing. (Would "good theology" raise the probability of healing, and conversely, would "bad theology" lower it?)
2. The expectation of being healed in the person in need. (If the person was expecting healing, would that increase the probability of healing?)
3. The training of the person in need. (If the person had already learned practical principles about healing, would that increase the probability?)
4. The previous experience with healing of the person in need. (If the person had prior knowledge of someone else being healed—whether family, friends, himself or herself, or some other reputable person—would the probability of healing be higher? Without previous experience, would the probability be lower?)
5. The use of commanding prayers regarding healing. (Would using commanding prayers increase the probability?)
6. Words of knowledge being given. (Would such words raise the probability?)

Independent variables 1, 3 and 4 proved to increase the probability of people with implanted metals in their bodies being healed. If the person in need of healing had a good, positive theology of healing, the probability went up. (Conversely, having a poor theology decreased the probability.) If the person in need had already received training on healing and had learned practical principles regarding healing, the probability also went up. And if the person had some previous experience with healing (either personally or in someone he or she knew), the probability went up. These three variables proved to be significant factors for those who were healed.

The remaining independent variables, 2, 5 and 6, did not show a higher probability of healing, but this was due in part to the faulty construct of the study, which caused a methodological confound. I know that all three of these variables—the expectation of a healing, using commanding prayer and receiving words of knowledge—do, in fact, increase the probability of healing. In the following analysis, let me briefly explain why they did not show up as significant factors in my doctoral research.

Independent variable 2, involving a person's expectation of being healed, is an enigma. One would have supposed this variable would be present with a preponderance of healings. Some people were surprised when they were healed, indicating that they were not expecting a healing. Others not only were surprised, but also felt unworthy. Others came to a meeting without expectations, but became expectant during the meeting. Those people may have answered the question about this variable by saying that they came in with little expectation, in contrast to the expectation that arose in them during the meeting.

Independent variable 5, using commanding prayer, was confounded by the fact that the percentage of people healed by commanding prayer was lower than one would expect during the services where the studies were conducted, simply because people had the opportunity to be healed by watching testimony videos first. The videos created faith in people, and at the end of the videos people were asked to see if they had already been healed prior to being prayed for. Most often, they were healed through watching the videos. Likewise, when asked to do something they could not do, people again were healed even before prayer. Then came the use of commanding prayers after all of that took place. The percentage of healings through the use of commanding prayer in those meetings would have been higher had there not been so many people healed earlier, before prayer for healing ever took place. This confound surprised me.

Independent variable 6, the word of knowledge variable, was confounded by the fact that specific words of knowledge were not part of this study. Even without specific words of knowledge, I already had a gift of faith for healing of people with surgically implanted materials, so instead of giving words of knowledge for this kind of healing, I showed testimonies and videos at my meetings. This meant that when the people were surveyed or interviewed afterward, there was little opportunity for them to report that words of knowledge were a significant factor. This may have conveyed the incorrect impression that words of knowledge are not highly connected to healing, when in fact they are—just not in the case of commanding prayer coming from the platform for people with implanted materials. During the last nineteen years of my ministry, words of knowledge have had a significant effect on the number of healings I have seen. At least 50 percent of the people who receive a healing in my meetings also receive words of knowledge for their condition prior to receiving their healing.

The Nature of Faith

During my doctoral study, much of my focus was on the nature of faith. The research I did for my thesis helped me in my thinking about faith, though not just any type of faith. Remember that in the previous chapter I talked about the different types of faith, including the God-infused, mountain-moving faith of God and the saving type of faith? I also talked about different degrees of faith. I want to discuss that mountain-moving type of faith a little further here. It is the kind of faith that relates to the supernatural, especially to healing and miracles. As I said earlier, it goes beyond faith *in* God, to having the faith *of* God—the gift of faith.

This kind of faith produces miracles, and it comes from God as a gift. It is not the kind of gift that is maintained or constituted; it is a situational gift given for the moment. Omar Cabrera spoke of this kind of faith being created in him by a light he would see over someone. He knew that when he saw this light, the person under the light would receive a miracle. William Branham encountered similar situations in which he would see a light over someone, and then a miracle would take place for that person. (Both men believed the light they saw was an angel.) Other times, Branham would have a vision beforehand that would create faith in him for the miraculous. At the point of the miracle, he would find himself exactly in the context of the vision and he would know just what to do, having witnessed the same scenario playing out in his vision earlier.

Sometimes God supplies faith to raise the dead through signs He gives to the one who is praying. In Mozambique, for example, God used a key leader and his wife in Iris Ministries[1] several times to raise the dead. When I interviewed this couple, they had been used to raise four people from the dead. Another relative of theirs also had been used to raise seven people from the dead.

I asked this leader, "Do you pray for all the dead?"

"Of course not," he responded. "It would be an embarrassment to the church to pray for all the dead."

"Then how do you know whom to pray for?" I asked. "When or how do you know when to pray for the dead?"

He responded, "While my wife is talking to the family, I place my hand on the dead person's foot or near the ankle. If the place where I am touching the dead person begins to become warm, or if I am praying for the person under my breath and I feel a large bolt of energy go through my body, then I give my wife a sign. She will then announce, 'We are going to pray for this person to be raised from the dead.' When we do this, we see people raised from the dead."

Here is another interesting illustration of the connection between revelation and faith. Through a gift of healing a woman near Uberlândia, Brazil, was healed of stage 4 terminal cancer. A friend of this woman with cancer had a bizarre dream. The friend was handed a coin in the dream and was told that when she met the man whose name was on the opposite side of the coin, her friend would be healed. When she turned the coin over in the dream, it had the name *Randy Clark* on it.

My name is not a Portuguese name, and this woman had never heard of me before. A few days after her dream, however, while she was driving through the city, she saw a flyer with my name on it, *Randy Clark*. It was announcing a meeting for healing that we were about to hold.

This woman who had had the dream came to our meeting, bringing her young friend with cancer along. The sick woman only had a few weeks to live due to her cancer. When the two of them told me the dream, it created a gift of faith in me. I was so confident that the woman would be healed of cancer that even though there were no indications of anything happening when I prayed, I persevered. I kept praying for her healing for over twenty minutes before the first indication of God's power began to touch her.

When God's power finally did touch her, it came with such intensity that she began to tremble and shake hard enough to bounce up and down on her seat. All the organs in her abdominal cavity were full of cancer, and so were the bones in her thighs. The heat in her legs was so intense that when she got up from her seat, her clothing underneath was wet. She was healed in a highly unusual manner. The heat and power would come on her for fifteen to twenty minutes, and then it would stop for about five minutes. Then the cycle would repeat all over again. She went through six cycles of healing that night.

The point of these illustrations is that this kind of faith comes from God as a gift. It is not an attainment, nor is it constant. It cannot be created by someone's confession or by some spiritual exercise. It is a gift that sometimes comes by a revelation of what God intends to do, and other times comes as its own gift, supplying unnatural faith for a mountain to move.

In whatever way the scriptural passages I talked about back in chapter 16 are translated—"have faith *in* God" or "have faith *of* God"—it still remains true that this type of faith has its source in God, not in the person who is praying. It is an altogether different type of faith than saving faith, although it is worth noting that even saving faith is a gift of prevenient grace that enables people to believe the Gospel.

Faith for the Moment

This mountain-moving faith is not normal faith that is in some way related to the faithfulness of God, as understood by the person praying. Instead, it is a situational gift of grace enabling the person to believe or have faith for a specific outcome in a specific moment. The best teacher on this aspect of faith was Dr. Charles Price, whom I introduced in an earlier chapter. He was the liberal pastor who was touched and healed in an Aimee Semple McPherson meeting. Dr. Price wrote,

> I call it [faith] a grace, because that is just what it is. In our blindness of heart and mind, we have taken faith out of the realm of the spiritual and, without realizing just what we were doing, have put it in the realm of the metaphysical. An army of emotions and desires has driven Faith from the chambers of the heart into the cold and unfruitful corridors of the mind. . . . *The*

revelation has answered my questions. . . . It has revolutionized my healing ministry, for it has revealed to me the helplessness of self; and the need for the presence, the love, the grace, and the faith, of *Jesus*.[2]

In his wisdom Dr. Price continues,

Remember that faith—the weight of the grain of mustard seed—will do more than a ton of will, or a mind full of determination. Genuine faith can no more manifest itself without result, than the sunshine without light and heat.

Knowing this, and believing it to be true, what is it that we have been mistakenly calling faith, because real faith never fails to bring about the result? In my own heart, I am satisfied that many of God's children have failed to behold the difference between faith and belief. To believe in healing is one thing; but to have faith *for* it is altogether something else.

Therein has been our difficulty. We have made faith a condition of mind when it is a divinely imparted grace of the heart.[3]

In his sermon "Till All Our Struggles Cease," Dr. Price continues to distinguish the nature of faith as being a gift from God, not human attainment in thought. He states,

One of the chief difficulties is our failure to see that faith can be received *only* as it is imparted to the heart, by God Himself. Either you have faith or you do not. You cannot manufacture it; you cannot work it up. You can believe a promise, and at the same time not have the faith to appropriate it. But we have formed the habit of trying to appropriate by *belief*: forgetting the while that *belief is a mental quality,* and that when we try to believe ourselves into an experience, we are getting into a metaphysical realm.[4]

In relation to prayer, Dr. Price, like Francis MacNutt, makes the distinction between intercessory prayer and prayers of command. MacNutt, a leading Catholic in healing ministry, wrote in his book *Healing* about the difference between intercessory or petitionary prayer and commanding prayer.[5] Dr. Price goes on to state,

> There may be a place for intercession, but it is not in the exercise of faith. Intercession and groaning of the heart may precede the operation of faith; *but when God's faith is imparted, the storm dies down and there is great calm and a deep settled peace in the soul.* The only sound will be the voice of thanksgiving and praise. The full realization—that it was not our ability to believe that made the sickness go, but rather that the faith which is of God was imparted . . .
>
> The mistake with many people has been that they have confused their own ability to believe for the faith that is of God. To sit down and repeat over and over, "I am healed—I am healed—I am healed" is not only unscriptural, but extremely dangerous spiritually.[6]

Dr. Price also discusses the connection between faith and belief:

> All things are possible *with God*. But Mark (9:23) tells us, "If thou canst believe, all things are possible to him that believeth." The belief that Jesus is speaking of here *is not head belief or mental acquiescence, but* that heart belief which is *faith*. This is proved by the account that Matthew gives of the story of the lunatic boy, to which we have already referred. In the account by Matthew, Jesus said, "If ye have faith as a grain of mustard seed;" while in the narrative recorded by Mark, "If ye believe." So the "belief" of Mark and the "faith" of Matthew are identical. That is my point. That is what the Spirit of God has been causing my poor eyes to behold *that faith is not intellectual, but spiritual*. It is primarily of heart—not of mind. Genuine, scriptural faith is not *our ability* to "count it done." It is the faith that only God can give.[7]

Charles Price was not the only one to hold to this understanding of faith and healing. So did F. F. Bosworth, William Branham and Omar Cabrera Sr. Today, Bill Johnson, Luke Truxel (a healing evangelist in Switzerland) and I all have the same understanding. But I quoted Dr. Price at length because I know of no other writer who has expressed this view as powerfully as he did. Furthermore, I believe the faith that moves mountains is this kind of faith. And I believe that Jesus and Paul would agree.

19

Practical Applications

Whatever you have learned or received or heard from
me, or seen in me—put it into practice. And the
God of peace will be with you.

Philippians 4:9

I have shared with you in the pages of this book many of the
insights I have gained over my years in healing ministry. We
first talked about the rubble we needed to clear away—all the
things that can get in the way of creating an atmosphere for
healing. Then we looked at some specific things we can teach
and implement to help usher in a healing breakthrough. We also
looked at some of the strong connections involved in healing
ministry. For example, the gifts of revelation and the gift of faith
are connected to increasing the measure of faith in a congregation. The gift of faith is also connected to seeing healings, and
particularly to seeing miracles.

While all those things have been important to cover, there
is yet another thing necessary to talk about if we are to reach
a healing breakthrough—practical applications. How can we

practically apply the insights we have learned about so that more people can experience the power of God to heal?

In answer to that question, I have developed the following strategy for use within a healing service. As you read through it, note that although you could vary the flow of a healing service so that it differs from what I give here, the practices I am about to recommend would almost always happen sometime during the service, and usually in the order that follows. Through much experience, I have found that the strategy I am going to share is highly effective in creating an atmosphere of faith in a congregation.

An Effective Order of Service

Most of the healing services I am invited to be part of begin with a time of praise and worship, followed by the pastor or leader introducing me and bringing me to the platform. At that point, the first thing I do is build an opening message around words of knowledge. I define what they are, and I explain their purpose and how they relate to healing by creating faith. Sometimes I tell the story of blind Bartimaeus, using it as an illustration of how a word of knowledge works. Jesus did not go to blind Bartimaeus, but instead sent one of His disciples with a message: "Cheer up! On your feet! He's calling you!" (Mark 10:49). Then I explain that the way Bartimaeus threw his cloak to the ground—the cloak that was his identification as *blind* Bartimaeus—was a sign of faith. It was like tearing up your Social Security disability card, because it was a special cloak the synagogue had given him to identify him as a legitimate beggar worthy of receiving people's alms.

The next thing I do is find someone near the front and ask him or her this question in front of the congregation: "If Jesus appeared to you and told you He wanted to heal you, would that affect you in any way?"

The person usually replies, "Yes!"

I follow that response with another question, "How would it affect you? Would you be feeling anything, or would you be excited?"

Again, the person usually responds with an enthusiastic "Yes!"

I follow up with another question: "Would you have faith that you would be healed?"

"Yes!"

"If it were Jesus Himself standing in front of you, would you have this excitement, this faith, even *before* you felt anything?"

"Yes!"

Then I make this final statement to the congregation: "When you understand that a word of knowledge involves a modern-day disciple bringing *Jesus'* message of *His* desire to heal you, the result should be the same experience of excitement and faith in you. That is why I'm taking the time to help you have a better understanding of words of knowledge and their relationship to healing."

Sometimes I follow this by illustrating how my wife, DeAnne, was instantly healed after watching people being healed in church for three days, primarily through words of knowledge. The following Sunday morning, the person who was ministering identified DeAnne's condition in a word of knowledge.

"This morning while I was taking a shower," this minister said, "the Lord told me he was going to heal someone with TMJ." (TMJ, or temporomandibular joint dysfunction, involves compromised movement and pain in the jaw joint and its surrounding muscles.)

On hearing this word about a healing for TMJ, DeAnne jumped out of her seat and yelled, "That's me!" She ran to the front of the church, and then felt suddenly embarrassed by the realization that the minister had not invited her to come to the front. Then she also realized that she had already been healed. No one, including the minister, had prayed for her. She had been healed by the faith the word of knowledge created in her.

These illustrations support my main message, which I usually base on Matthew 4:17 (NIV1984): "From that time on Jesus began to preach, 'Repent, for the kingdom of heaven is near.'" My actual sermon is only about five or ten minutes long, but the time I spend explaining other things related to healing takes almost an hour. I explain words of knowledge, and I also explain why I ask people to wave their hands when they are 80 percent healed rather than 100 percent. Additionally, at some point I usually make faith declarations about what I expect will happen in the meeting. These declarations of faith are not hype; they are my honest, genuine expectations based on my history with God and what I have seen Him do in past meetings.

After the teaching, I usually show some testimony videos. I ask after each video that the people present who have similar issues try to do what they could not do before. I have them test their bodies to see if they have been healed. (Many are healed during the videos, even before anyone prays for them.) I then pray for those who have an issue similar to what they saw on the video, but who are not yet healed. More people are healed during that prayer.

After the videos, I begin to give words of knowledge and pray for the people who stand up to indicate that they have the condition I called out. I then have the team come to the stage to join me, and they also give words of knowledge. When larger teams of more than 25 people are with me, I instruct them to give only their strongest word of knowledge. Then if time permits, they can give their second-strongest word of knowledge.

After we pray for those who are standing in response to the words of knowledge, we inspect the results by asking those whose condition has improved by at least 80 percent to wave both hands over their heads. We follow this by asking those who are not yet 80 percent better—but who are getting better—to wave one hand. Then we pray for this group again, and again repeat our inspection to see who was healed during the second prayer.

Sometime during this process of giving words of knowledge and praying, I make a request that those with substantial healings come to the platform to give their testimony. I usually limit this to from 5 to 15 people (or on some occasions, no more than 25). The last thing I do from the platform is ask those people to stand who came to the meeting in need of prayer, believing that they would be healed. Then I ask for those people to stand who came *not* expecting healing, but who now would like prayer because their faith has increased through witnessing what God is doing in the meeting. I pray a final prayer for this group and again call for them to inspect their bodies to see if function has been restored by 80 percent or more, or if their pain has decreased by that amount. After each prayer, there is a counting of all healed over 80 percent, and it is reported to the church.

The ministry team then comes down off the platform to the floor to face the crowd, so the team members are ready to minister to those who will come forward for prayer with the laying on of hands. I instruct the team and the church to indicate when people receive at least an 80 percent improvement by clapping their hands together loudly fifteen times. The number healed is added to the total and announced the next night.

The remainder of the congregation is then dismissed to leave whenever they would like. During this time of prayer, those on the team who see a major healing in someone are to bring that person to the platform for an interview on camera. The most powerful testimonies are then given from the platform over the mic.

The 80 Percent Indicator

What I have given you here is not an iron-clad order of service. I do sometimes change it. I should also mention that I have a specific reason that I ask people to stand if their condition is called out in a word of knowledge, and to wave one hand if they began to feel anything. I explain to them that it is to build faith instead of doubt. I tell them that if words of knowledge are given and no one stands, choosing instead to wait until the end, it can cause an atmosphere of skepticism or doubt to come into the room. The same thing is true if they do not wave a hand as soon as they feel something happening. Delaying their response to words of knowledge can rob God of His glory because it can cause people to think, *This person giving a word is not hearing from God; he's missing it. God is not in this.*

On the other hand, if people stand up as soon as their condition is called out, it causes faith to rise in the room. As they stand up when they hear the word and start waving their hand as soon as they feel something, it builds an atmosphere of faith for a healing breakthrough.

I also have a reason that I ask people to wave both hands when they are at least 80 percent healed. I explain to the congregation that they are to wave both hands at 80 percent—not wait for 100 percent healing—because that, too, builds faith in the congregation. When the people around them see what God is doing in those few seconds immediately after a prayer for healing, faith rises. But if those who are being healed wait until their healing is 100 percent complete to raise their hands, it leaves a time span where very few people are raising their hands and a spirit of skepticism can arise. If no one realizes how much healing has already gone on during that delayed response time, unbelief can start to build instead of faith, even though many of the people present have already been healed by 80, 90, 95 or even 98 percent.

On the other hand, if I lower the percentage to 80 percent healed (which is still a substantial amount) and tell people to wave both hands when they reach that level of healing, I find many more people will indicate much sooner that God is in the process of healing them. When the congregation sees this response in the few seconds following a prayer for healing, their expectation for healing rises exponentially. And within that atmosphere of faith, we see a breakthrough and more healings begin to occur. You can see how all these applications work together to build faith in a healing service.

Issues with Implanted Materials

What I have given you is the order of service I follow on the first night of a series of healing meetings that lasts three or four nights. But if you have only a one-night meeting scheduled, this order still works well. When I have more than one night to work with, each subsequent night builds on the foundation I laid during the first night's teaching. The amount of time I give to teaching diminishes after that first night. The second night I often teach on the power of the testimony. The third night I teach again on some aspect of healing, and I allow more time for testimonies. On the final night I show two or three videos of people being healed from complications due to implanted materials.

Before any testimony videos about people with metal in their bodies being healed, I remind the congregation that there could be people healed simply by watching the video with an expectation of healing. I tell them that almost always, people are healed just watching the video. My expectation for this is so high that I tell the crowd that immediately following the video, there will be an inspection to see who has been healed by at least 80 percent. This also raises their expectation for healing.

Following a video, I tell the congregation, "Check out your body to see if your pain levels have gone down by at least 80 percent. Also see if your range of motion has been restored by at least 80 percent. If you are at 80 percent or more healed, stand and wave both hands over your head." (By this time in the service, they understand the concept of giving God glory when they are 80 percent healed, since I already explained it when I taught about words of knowledge.)

Finally, I invite those who have waved their hands to come to the platform and give their testimonies. The questions I ask them are designed to keep building faith in the congregation, so that even at that late point we will continue to see people being healed. What follows are the questions I ask. (These questions are also applicable not only to testimonies about metal, but also to other healing testimonies.)

"What was wrong with you before you were healed? What couldn't you do before that you now can do?"

"How much pain were you in before you were healed, on a scale of 0–10, with 0 being no pain and 10 being excruciating pain? What is your pain level now that you are healed?"

"Did you feel anything prior to your healing, for example heat, energy, electricity or coldness?"

"When were you healed? Was it while watching the testimony video, or when you stood in response to a word of knowledge, or during prayer for healing, or when you tried to do what you could not do before?"

Usually, these "live" healing testimonies build even more faith in those who are present, so that as we offer a final prayer in conclusion at the end of the service, even more people are healed.

Applying What Works

The practices I have listed in this chapter are all steps you can take to build people's faith when you minister healing in a service. I have found that these practical applications work well.

If you are the one being prayed for rather than the one ministering, reading about these practices will give you an understanding of how important your response is to what God is doing. If you need healing, don't delay if a word of knowledge is given about your condition or if you feel something starting to happen. Respond quickly and with thanksgiving to what God is doing, follow the direction of those who are ministering and give God praise and glory even before your healing is complete. Thank Him for the measure of healing you received, but continue to ask for complete healing. When you receive complete healing, express your thanksgiving to Him and tell others about your healing, which is also important.

If you are the one ministering healing, declare in faith what you expect will happen in a service. This is not hype, of course, but a genuine expectation based on your history with God. Explain the power and purpose of words of knowledge clearly, and explain how the congregation should respond to them. Encourage people to respond with excitement to what God is doing as soon as they feel something happening, and have them give God glory before their healing is even complete. Invite the power of the testimony into the service, both in the form of video testimonies and in live testimonies given by those present who are healed.

Practical applications such as these will result in a greater belief among the people that God is in their midst, healing those in need. And that atmosphere of faith will result in a healing breakthrough.

Contending for Breakthrough

Is anyone among you sick? Let them call the elders of the church to pray over them and anoint them with oil in the name of the Lord. And the prayer offered in faith will make the sick person well; the Lord will raise them up. If they have sinned, they will be forgiven.

James 5:14–15

When you pray for someone and the person is healed, it can be quite rewarding. On the other hand, when you pray for someone and he or she is not healed, it can be extremely frustrating. Yet there are hindrances that can stand in the way of healing, and it is often necessary to contend for a healing breakthrough.

Remember that in your healing prayer ministry, you likely will see a variety of results. You may see people who are 100 percent healed. You may see people who are 80 percent or more healed, but who are continuing to believe and receive prayer for complete healing. You may see some who are healed less than 80 percent. You may encounter others who are not healed at all—yet. Whatever your results, it is important to remember that you must continue to press in. You must keep believing that God is a God who still heals. It is also important to encourage those whom you are praying for and with to hold on to this mindset.

You may be wondering what hinders healing prayer. I encourage you to press in to the Holy Spirit for direction about whatever is hindering your healing or the healing of someone else for whom you are praying. Some common hindrances include fear, unforgiveness, spiritual warfare and people's sense that they have caused their own health problems through their lifestyle choices.

While that last one may be true to some extent, even when people repent and are willing to change their ways, they can still feel unworthy of healing. The best solution to this major obstacle is to help them understand grace by reasoning with them from Scripture, so that they move from fearing justice into receiving grace. We can work through various hindrances to healing, and we can pray against and break them. It is up to those of us in healing ministry to walk people through whatever may be a hindrance, so that they can receive complete healing.

"Losing" a Healing

One of the frustrations of healing ministry is that you may pray for people who are either partially or fully healed, and then you may find out later that they feel they have "lost" their healing. They may feel it is fully gone, or they may feel they are not doing as well as they were when they first were healed.

"Losing" a healing can happen for a variety of reasons. One reason is that people may have a wavering level of faith. They may be overcome with worry about what could happen to them if their healing is lost. By focusing on the worry, they allow the enemy to get in and their symptoms or affliction to return.

Another reason people may lose their healing is that they do not change the lifestyle they were living before the healing occurred. For example, suppose that due to an injury a man favored his right leg prior to healing. After the healing, if he continues to walk the way he is used to and favors that leg, it could cause the healing to dissipate because of his lack of a lifestyle change.

Or suppose that someone has respiratory problems due to smoking. The person could receive healing for the problem, but if he or she continues smoking, the problem will return.

Another example would be someone who develops diabetes or gout related to an unhealthy diet. The person may get healed, but if the diet does not change, the diabetes or gout will return. (Some diabetes is caused by a genetic propensity toward the disease and is unrelated to diet. That would be a different situation.)

If there is a clear connection between people's sickness or disease and their lifestyle, I do not recommend making an issue of it prior to healing prayer. This could reinforce the obstacle of them thinking, *I deserve my sickness because of what I have done to my body.* (It also is not helpful when people think that you are judging them.) Instead, wait until after healing prayer, and then discuss the importance of making lifestyle changes. It can be hard for people to change their patterns once their behavior is set in everyday life, but these lifestyle changes are crucial for people to make in walking out their healing.

Difficult as it may be for those of us who are ministering healing, it is important that we speak up about these lifestyle issues during what I call in my Five-Step Prayer Model the post-prayer suggestion time, after we have finished praying for someone. For example, if the cause of someone's sickness was unforgiveness, it would be important to tell the person to guard his or her heart and be quick to forgive after the healing. If the cause of someone's sickness was an afflicting spirit, it would be important to tell the person to use his or her authority in Christ to rebuke any symptoms such a spirit may try to bring back upon the body.

Fear is another reason that people may not be healed or may lose their healing. People may be afraid of change, or they may have deeper issues they have not dealt with that they are afraid to face. Sometimes, you may want to recommend that the person you are praying for seek inner healing. Physical afflictions often are tied to emotional hurts that a person has not dealt with effectively. Dealing with emotional and spiritual afflictions can often help people receive full physical healing. Once emotional oppression is broken off, people can be liberated and be free to receive the physical healing that is rightly theirs.

Sometimes, a lack of support can be behind someone losing a healing. Provide people with emotional support when you are praying for healing and even after your prayer is through. This is important both for people who have already been healed and for those who have not yet been healed. Remind them all to press in to the Lord, keep focused on God, stay in the Word and seek spiritual support from the Body of Christ. Encourage them in tangible ways to walk out their healing or faith for healing.

Some tangible ways to encourage people might include reminding them that God's power is greater than their affliction or symptom, sometimes even to a point beyond our natural understanding. For example, it might be difficult for people to grasp fully that God can heal an affliction that they have been told is incurable or hopeless. Or if they have been dealing with some kind of chronic affliction that they have had for decades, it might be hard for them to believe that the problem really could be removed for good. Encourage them that God can and does heal in those situations. Encourage them that once they are healed, they really can stay healed permanently. They do not need to lose their healing for any reason. In fact, they need to guard against losing it.

Also remind people that although God still heals, His timing may be different than what we want. But we must trust that He can heal us. In certain situations where people seem as though they are not ready or willing to receive prayer or even gain an understanding of God's ability to heal, it can be helpful to pray for their encouragement.

Getting Healing and Staying Healed

Whether or not people believe God can heal directly affects their level of expectation. I have seen many different levels of expectation in my meetings. Many times, people's expectations affect whether or not they get healed or keep their healing. Keeping focused on God is helpful in getting healed and staying healed. So is being exposed to healing testimonies, either live or through books or videos. So is studying God's Word. All these things serve to remind people that healing *can* and *does* happen.

Whether you are in healing ministry or are the person in need of healing, renew your mind by reading Scriptures that pertain to healing. Several times I have taken my Bibles and marked all the passages that deal with healing, so that I can quickly read those passages. That is a good way to keep the enemy at bay and keep your heart focused on God. God's Word is yours to keep, so stand firm in it and resist the enemy.

Press in for complete, 100 percent healing. Focus on the healing that has happened already, not just the healing you are still waiting for. When praying for your healing or someone else's, command in the name of Jesus that the affliction be gone. What

God promised in Jesus' time is still happening today! If someone you are praying for is healed of leg pain but is still experiencing jaw pain, remind the person to focus on the leg being healed, not on the jaw pain. Focusing on what God has done will keep the person's mind on what God still can do.

Building each other up and supporting each other are also important factors in getting healed and staying healed. As I said, a lack of support can cause issues with healing. A co-author of mine, Craig Miller, tells this story in our book *Finding Victory When Healing Doesn't Happen*:

> There was a woman that lived alone and was unable to travel outside her home because of her debilitating neurological condition. When my wife and I prayed every other week for God to bring healing for the pain, swelling, shaking, and numbness in her arms and legs, she would feel and walk better each time we finished prayer. When we met with her the next time she would be emotionally discouraged and had reverted back to the physical condition that we prayed during our prior visit. At first we were baffled as to why she was not keeping her healing from one visit to the next. After several visits we came to realize she had no support in between our visits to encourage her. She could only rely on her own thoughts and ability and could not sustain what she had gained the week before. In situations of poor support it is important to explore ways to connect people with resources such as phone calls, visits, prayer lines, greeting cards, emails, and any other ways to keep the person encouraged.[1]

To create faith and build up the type of atmosphere that sees a greater numbers of healings, encourage people by actively listening to their afflictions. Confirm that you understand what they have been through or are going through, and let them know that you understand where they hope to go from where they are. Encourage and support them both before and after their healing. It will build their faith both to get healed and to stay healed.

Resting in the Promise

The more you work with people to believe that God *can* and *does* heal today, the more you will see healings happen. Encourage the people who might be ministering healing with you that they have the authority in Christ to pray for healing. Encourage those whom you are praying for that healing is a promise from God.

While praying, be aware of and pray against any hindrances to healing. Bind any negative spirits and pray for a greater presence of God's Spirit. Keep yourself and others focused on what is greater. In other words, focus on the healing, not on the symptoms or afflictions. This is crucial for anyone who has been healed or who has faith for healing.

Remember, God loves us and *wants* us to get healed and stay healed. He desires health for us. He promises it. According to Matthew, who was quoting Isaiah 53:4, Christ "took up our infirmities and bore our diseases" (Matthew 8:16–17). Jesus carried our sicknesses, and "by His stripes we are healed" (Isaiah 53:5 NKJV). We all can rest in that promise.

21

Handling Unanswered Prayer for Healing

Rejoice always, pray continually, give thanks in all circumstances; for this is God's will for you in Christ Jesus.

1 Thessalonians 5:16–18

I was sixteen when the question of why some people are healed and others are not became not just a theological issue, but also a personal issue for me. I knew that God had healed my Grandma Ray of a large goiter in her throat, and I was aware that my Sunday school teacher, Immogene, had been healed of cancer. But then when I was a teen, my Grandpa Ray had discovered he had cancer. He could not urinate without great difficulty, and upon examination the doctors discovered he had prostate cancer. He was 61 years old. Tragically, by the time it was discovered, the cancer had metastasized to his colon and into his bones.

I remember going into Grandpa Ray's room after his colostomy surgery. He asked if I wanted to see the colostomy, and I said yes. The next thing I knew, I had passed out and was seated in a chair. For years I had been making fun of my dad, who had almost passed out a few times when I had been injured. Somehow I had become like my dad.

I loved Grandpa Ray very much. We were a close family, with both sets of grandparents living within four miles of our home. We would go to visit Grandpa and Grandma Clark one weekend and Grandpa and Grandma Ray the next weekend. It seemed as though we were visiting the grandparents every Sunday.

During Grandpa Ray's cancer battle I got my driver's license, so I would sometimes drive him to his cancer treatments. I remember him being in great pain from the bone cancer, and I would massage his back as best I could. Grandpa's cancer was aggressive. He had been a chain smoker most of his life, smoking two to three packs of unfiltered Camels a day. He did not eat a healthy diet, either. But in fairness, the early warnings of cancer and tobacco being connected were just coming out in the 1960s, and initially a lot of people did not believe the surgeon general's warnings were true.

Grandpa's fight with cancer quickly became a losing battle. My family sent out word for Christians to be praying for his healing. The same local church that had prayed for my Sunday school teacher prayed for Grandpa. Many other churches also prayed for his healing, yet it just did not happen.

This created my first theological crisis. Why did God heal Grandma Ray and my Sunday school teacher, but not Grandpa Ray? Grandpa was a lovely Christian. He had been gloriously saved out of alcoholism about fourteen years earlier. He had experienced a powerful conversion and had become a transformed man—radically different. He was devout, a man of prayer and a lover of God. He fought to live, but in just about a year he died.

Why? Why wasn't he healed? I asked myself. I did not understand. His death made heaven an even dearer place to me. I would console myself in my grief by contemplating that life was truly short and that I would see Grandpa again when I died and went to heaven. Our circle would be unbroken.

Healing was such a mystery, and I did not have the answers. I did develop the belief that in order to be healed, you had to be *very* close to Jesus, the way my Grandma Ray and my Sunday school teacher were. In my young teenage mind, they were almost in the category of sainthood in their relationship to God. The only thing I could figure out was that Grandpa must not have been holy enough to merit healing.

Of course, the theological reasonings of my sixteen-year-old mind were unbiblical. Actually, healing was a subject that was never taught in my General Baptist denominational background. Healing was believed possible in answer to intercessory prayer, but there was no belief in gifts of healing or healers for today or the working of miracles. There was no exposure to Pentecostal, Holiness or Word of Faith theologies of healing in the General Baptist churches I attended. Instead, there was soft cessationism teaching. The mindset was that although the gifts of healing did not exist, people could be healed in response to intercessory prayer. Healing was not normative; it was thought of as exceptional. But occasionally it did occur. In such a theological environment, strong, expectant faith was hard to find.

The theology of holiness that I had come up with—that extreme holiness was required for healing to occur—was destroyed two years later. I was in a serious car accident, and afterward I was healed of life-threatening injuries. This happened just four days after I had rededicated my life to the Lord, so clearly I had not had enough time to get into what I thought of as a holy enough condition to merit being healed. Four days earlier, I had been living a sinful, hypocritical life, and I had been living that way for the past eleven months before the accident.

I knew I was not living a holy life when I was healed, so now my theology of healing was really confused. Apparently, healing was not necessarily related to the issue of holiness. Otherwise, I would not have been healed. But because I had been healed, the subject of healing became a very important theological and practical issue for me, especially since I received my call into ministry within one month of my healing.

Rejecting Liberal Theology

My theological education was liberal. I entered Oakland City College and majored, minored and took all my electives in religious studies. I had been raised in fundamentalist churches that were dispensational and quasi-cessational, and that believed in a pre-tribulation rapture. My college professors were all quite liberal, so much so that I began to have serious theological questions about my faith. By the time I graduated college, I did not believe in angels, demons or nature miracles like the instant withering of the tree when Jesus cursed it, or the way He calmed the storm and walked on water.

I began questioning so much about my faith. I realized that my education had nearly destroyed it. I knew I needed to resolve my theological issues. For this reason I decided to go to The Southern Baptist Theological Seminary in Louisville, Kentucky. I really wanted to go to a much more conservative Methodist seminary, Asbury Seminary in Wilmore, Kentucky, but I could not attend there for two reasons. First, I could not afford it. It was three or four times more expensive than the Baptist seminary. Second, there was a rule at Asbury that if you spoke in tongues you could not become a student.

My plan was to try to find the most conservative professors at the Baptist seminary and play devil's advocate against them.

I would use the liberal arguments I already knew so well in the classroom, hoping the professors would give me answers that would destroy these arguments in my mind. I wanted answers to the questions that were causing me to have so much doubt and so little faith.

In seminary, however, even though I took the classes taught by the most conservative professors, there were many more professors who were even more liberal than the professors I had encountered in college. What kept me from losing my Christian faith entirely was that I could never doubt the supernatural nature of my own healing after my car accident.

Then, in my last year of seminary, two things occurred that helped me rebuild my faith. The first was that I got special permission to write a term paper on healing. The course was on the book of Acts, and we were given about fifty topics we could choose from. Healing was not on the list. I went to the professor and asked for permission to write on the subject of healing instead. He granted me permission, with the caveat that I could not simply use anecdotal stories. I had to do real research. I complied, and after I turned in my paper, he met with me to discuss it.

"I've never interacted with a student's paper as much as I have with yours," he told me. "You've written as if healing is central to the Gospel, and it is not. It is only peripheral to the Gospel."

"I strongly disagree," I told him. "I believe that healing is central to the Gospel!"

The research I did for this term paper was an eye-opener for me. It showed me how prejudiced theological schools were toward healing at that time (although many are somewhat better now), and how unscholarly they were in what they presented about healing. Writing that paper was an important catalyst for what would later happen in my life in regard to the healing ministry.

The second thing that helped me regain a strong faith was taking the course Biblical Authority and the Modern Mind.

This was one of the most liberal seminary courses I took in all of my theological training. One book I had to read for it helped me understand more clearly the presuppositions and worldview on which liberalism rests. As I read it, I realized that I did not agree with liberalism's deistic, anti-supernatural worldview, and I no longer believed liberalism's presuppositions had any logical consistency.

What caused me to reject liberalism's closed-universe, deistic, anti-supernatural position? My personal healing. My experience of healing contradicted liberalism's arguments and eventually became the anchor of my faith. Yet even though healing became so very important to my faith, I did not understand it. At that point in my life, I knew that my theology of healing was insufficient. I determined that I *must* learn more about healing. I knew healing happened, but it was such a mystery to me. I knew I needed to develop a better understanding of healing and the gifts of the Holy Spirit.

Healing in My First Pastorate

When I graduated from seminary at 25, I moved from being a student pastor to being a full-time pastor. In my first pastorate I would visit every parishioner who entered the hospital, every day that they were in the hospital. Back when I was 19 my pastor and mentor, Rev. Billy Duncan, had trained me in making hospital calls. I had served him as assistant pastor of the First General Baptist Church in McLeansboro, Illinois, but this was years later and I was on my own. It did not take me long to realize that I had not learned enough from him.

On every visit I read the Bible to the hospitalized. I knew which texts seemed to best fit their situations. I had learned this much from Rev. Duncan. He was an excellent pastor, in my opinion the best in our association of churches. I also prayed for each person prior to leaving the hospital room, or I prayed in the person's home if he or she was convalescing. But the day came when I began to analyze more critically what I was doing. I realized that my prayers were addressed more to the ears of the sick person than to God. I did begin and end my prayers by focusing on God, but what I was praying was not so much about people being healed, but more about them being comforted and being better able to cope with their sickness. There was no expectation for miraculous intervention attached to my prayers. I was praying to comfort the afflicted as they either naturally regained their health or ultimately died.

After six years of pastoring, two situations arose that began to change my approach to healing prayer. One was a sermon series on healing that I did based on Francis MacNutt's book *Healing*, which I mentioned earlier. This was an important sermon series for me because it helped me develop a better theology for healing. During this series, I began to pray for the sick differently. I was so excited when a woman was healed of two separate problems on two separate occasions. Then I realized that I had been duped. The woman was faking the healings for attention! I was so crushed and humiliated by this experience that I backed away from healing. I stopped praying for the sick with the laying on of hands for a whole year.

The second situation that changed my approach and brought it back around to praying with the laying on of hands involved the brother-in-law of the chairman of our deacon board. This man was dying of cancer, and I had been asked to go pray for him. He was not a member of my church, but out of love and respect for the chairman, whom I greatly respected, I went to visit his brother-in-law. I discovered that when I prayed for him along with laying my hands on his body, his pain would subside greatly. This lessened sense of pain happened every time I prayed for him, and it would continue for some time after the prayer. His condition continued to deteriorate, however, and over the months to come the cancer advanced. I continued to pray for him and every time, his pain would subside again, as if he had been given a morphine shot. But finally, the last time I saw him, I did not pray for his healing. I prayed that he would have peace in his transition from this life into the next. He died a few hours after that prayer.

I had conducted many funerals in my thirteen years of pastoring up until that time. I felt happy that I was able to help people with their grief over the death of a loved one. My sermons for grieving families focused on hope. I would talk about their loved ones entering their reward in Christ, the cessation of pain from illness or the limitations of old age, the joy of having a glorified body, and the glorious reception their loved ones would experience in heaven. I was actually pumped by the hope those who die in Christ have.

For all of my focus on the positives, when a funeral involved the death of a young person, especially if he or she had died of disease, it always caused a theological conundrum for me. I did not believe it was God's intentional will for someone to die so young. I even became angry when I would hear other pastors trying to comfort young parents by telling them, "God was making a bouquet in heaven and needed a rosebud to put into His bouquet, so He took your daughter."

Such pastoral answers angered me. I remember thinking, *If I were a grieving parent, that kind of pastoral response would make me want to tell that minister to get out of my house!* There was no comfort for me, no theological resolution in such pastoral responses to untimely deaths. Today, I still cannot accept that the sovereignty of God is the primary answer for the death of young people due to disease or accident. I prefer to see it from the perspective of a "two kingdoms at war" worldview.

Instead of attributing bad things to God, I believe the source of natural evil is the evil one, the devil. I believe disease is related to the Fall, and though there is some cause and effect related to lifestyle, there is also a sense that disease is not from God. It is somehow rooted in Satan, the demonic and our fallen human nature. This includes sinful lifestyles that contribute directly to disease, and the compromising of the immune system that results in sickness.

The "Whys" and "Why Nots"

Now that I have given you the big picture of my theological learning process about healing and my growth into healing ministry, it will be obvious to you that not every question has been answered for me along the way. There remain many questions about healing—and the lack of healing—that I still contend with after more than three decades of being involved in this type of prayer.

Why does a person with more than one health issue receive a major healing in one area, but not in another? Why does one person get healed of a certain physical problem, while another person with the same issue goes unhealed? Why do some people, like my Grandma Ray and my Sunday school teacher, get miraculously healed, while others, like my Grandpa Ray, ultimately die of their illnesses?

It is important to recognize that sometimes healing—or the lack of it—will remain a mystery. Our ability to move forward in healing ministry can depend on whether or not we can deal with that reality.

How do we handle unanswered prayer for healing? We must be able to continue building an atmosphere of faith for healing, while at the same time reconciling ourselves to the fact that questions we cannot answer this side of heaven still remain. Let's look at some stories of unanswered healings and talk about how we can reconcile ourselves to them and still move forward.

One Problem Healed, One Not . . .

Several years before the revival in Toronto, I was conducting a healing meeting hosted by a Roman Catholic church, but also promoted by area Protestants. In that meeting we experienced a woman's unusual, miraculous healing after I received a word of knowledge about a heart. The word came, and then shortly afterward I noticed a pastor friend's wife praying for a woman. The woman was breathing rapidly and moving her arms back and forth in coordination with her breathing. This was quite a noticeable demonstration, so I went over to check out what was going on.

"What's happening?" I asked.

"She has a terrible heart," the pastor's wife said. "She can only walk four or five feet without feeling exhausted and winded. She had been on a list for a heart transplant, and she had a friend drive her here from over a hundred miles away."

During prayer, the power of God began to come upon this woman's body powerfully. This was why her breathing was so pronounced, and why she was waving her arms. Then the healing came. She was healed! She rose up from the pew and ran around the sanctuary, up and down the steps, and out into the parking lot. It was a total healing.

Upon returning home, she was examined by her attending physician. He was the one who had told her that she needed a new heart and had put her on the heart transplant list.

Now he told her, "You have a new heart! This is not the heart I examined before."

It was an amazing healing, but what confused me was what I heard from her later on. I followed up with her some time later, after she had moved to Arizona.

"I had to move out here," she said, "because I still have severe arthritis and the climate helps me."

This woman had been totally healed of her heart problem and had been able to avoid having a heart transplant. Yet she still had severe arthritis and had to move to Arizona because of it. It was a mystery to me how the power of God could come so demonstrably and strongly on a person's body and cause a major healing of one problem, while at the same time not touching another problem.

I have determined that whatever the result of healing prayer, I will be faithful to the commands of the Great Commission, especially the second part, teaching the disciples we make to obey everything Jesus has commanded us (see Matthew 28:18–20). My obedience is not conditional on my ability to understand, but rather on my willingness to obey. I realize that the command to heal the sick and cast out demons is at the top (or near the top) of Jesus' commandments. If I had to wait until I understood these mysteries before I prayed for the sick, I would not have been praying for the sick these past thirty-plus years.

And what about the person who is sick, not just the person praying for the sick? If you are the one in need of healing, I recommend that you to continue to receive prayer. Even if you have been prayed for scores of times or hundreds of times, continue receiving prayer. I have encountered many people who had been prayed for numerous times without being healed. But because they did not give up and continued to receive prayer, they experienced healing.

One such person was a woman who had been prayed for many times for her multiple sclerosis (MS). She had had MS for ten years, and when it came to the point that she was in a wheelchair, she told her husband that they needed serious prayer for her healing. When she came to our meeting, God orchestrated events in the meeting that caused her faith to rise. It started with a friend of hers who came up to her and told her she would be healed. Then the testimonies and videos encouraged and strengthened her faith. Because she had metal in her body (a pain pump supplying morphine), she tried to stand in response to a word of knowledge about metal. At first she could not do it, and then God began to cause electricity to flow through her legs and arms, allowing her to stand up. Then she was healed of multiple problems—her MS, her herniated fourth and fifth lumbar vertebrae, her painful bladder syndrome and her permanent cognitive disability due to fourteen lesions on her brain. She is only one example of the many people I have met who had become disillusioned after many prayers for healing, but who did not give up and ultimately were healed.

A Minister's Father Unhealed

Bill Johnson is a dear friend of mine. He is a fellow minister who contends for breakthroughs in healing, as I do. Bill has shared with me the mystery regarding healing that his family faced. (He also gave me permission to share this story with you here.) Bill's father, Melvin Earl Johnson, was Bill's greatest cheerleader. He was also the pastor of Bethel Assembly of God in Redding, California, from 1968–1982. Earl was a progressive pastor and a great father to his children, all of whom are in ministry today.

I remember the day Bill received word that his father had discovered he had cancer. Bill was with me in Brazil, and he immediately returned home with my blessings. During the ensuing months, Earl Johnson received prayer from many who were noted for healing ministry. I was among them on more than one occasion. The family did all they knew of to seek healing. Earl was a man of great faith, as was his wife. All the members of his family were in ministry, and many of them had seen numerous people healed under their ministry. Nonetheless, Earl was not healed of the cancer and did not survive it.

During the last days of his life, Earl's family surrounded him with constant company, prayer and worship. Though their prayers for healing were unanswered, they did not allow this mystery to cause them to stop worshiping God. They were in worship when Earl slipped from this world into the spiritual world, where he instantly was relieved of his pain and received eternal life.

While the Johnson family was fighting this battle against Earl's cancer on every front, several people in the church experienced healing of the exact same kind of cancer that Earl had. The sermon Bill Johnson gave the Sunday after his father died is the most powerful response I can give here to what this chapter is about—the mystery of healing, and what to do when you are disappointed that the person being prayed for is unhealed (whether it is you or someone you are ministering to in prayer).

Bill made this powerful statement in that sermon: "Only on earth, in this situation, could I stand and offer worship to God while I am disappointed. I could never do this in heaven, because in heaven there is no disappointment. Only here can I offer a *sacrifice* of praise."

As pastors who believe in healing, Bill, Earl and so many of us have experienced so much mystery that we don't understand. We see the power of God come and perform amazing healings, but we are left with so many unanswered questions regarding the ministry of healing and those who go unhealed. How do we handle unanswered prayer for healing? I could not have said it better than Bill did in his sermon. We can handle it by accepting that the mystery remains, and by offering God a sacrifice of praise.

More Mystery Stories

The director of the Global Awakening school that focuses on supernatural ministry shared with me a mystery he experienced while he was pastoring a Mennonite church in Illinois. A woman in his church had multiple sclerosis (MS), and she was in the last stages of the disease. She and her husband were regular volunteers at the food ministry. In this capacity she would pray for people who came for food, but who also were experiencing health problems.

This woman had lost the ability to move her arms, so when she began to pray for people, her husband would lift her arm with his hand and put it on the area of a person's sickness. Often, people were healed after this woman with MS prayed for them. My director friend said that he saw this happen hundreds of times with her. The power for healing would flow into the sick as she prayed for them, but seemed to bypass her even as it flowed through her. She was never healed of her MS.

Years ago while I was pastoring full-time, one of the key group leaders in my church found out that his wife had leukemia. A few years earlier, we had already had one young woman with leukemia die from the common cold during a bone marrow transplant. Now the congregation was facing leukemia again as the disease attacked one of the most beloved young women in our church. I will call her Jenee and her husband Darrel.

Jenee and Darrel had one daughter who loved them both dearly, along with a church full of people who loved them. This couple and our whole church waged a gallant fight against Jenee's leukemia and contended mightily for her healing. She had an intimate relationship with God, referring to him as "Daddy God," and they were key group leaders in the church. During the battle for her life, the church went on a forty-day fast where someone was fasting for each of the forty days. In addition, some of the people fasted the whole forty days individually as they cried out in prayer for Jenee's healing.

On a daily basis, teams of people went either to the couple's home or to the hospital to pray for Jenee. This went on until the day she came to church shortly before she died. Her health and frequent long hospitalizations had kept her from coming very much during her illness. She looked like a skeleton wrapped in skin. Her body reflected the losing battle it had been waging.

People were so shaken by Jenee's appearance that some came to my wife and said, "We need to stop praying for Jenee and let her go to heaven!"

I was in Japan at that time, ministering healing and impartation in Tokyo. DeAnne called and told me what was happening. She asked me what I thought we should do.

"What would you want our church to do if it were me in Jenee's place?" I asked my wife.

DeAnne replied, "I would want the church to fight for you until you died, and then I would want them to pray for you to be raised from the dead. I would want them to do everything possible."

"Okay, then go back and ask Darrel and Jenee what they would want the church to do for them," I responded. "Do they want the church to keep praying for her healing, or do they want to stop fighting?"

When DeAnne asked Darrel and Jenee what they wanted the church to do, they said, "We want you to fight! Don't stop praying for healing!"

So that is what we did until the day Jenee died. We fought the best fight we knew how to fight, but she did not live. She was received in heaven, having fought a good fight. We were left wrestling with the mystery of it.

From a pastoral perspective, it is difficult to understand that sometimes you pray for someone who does not seem to have any faith or expectancy for healing, yet they are healed. And other times you see one of your best, most dedicated members lose the fight against an illness. The deceased person was full of faith yet went unhealed, while during the same time period you watched someone who did not seem to be nearly as "good" a Christian be healed of the same condition in response to prayer. In times like that, disappointment has to give way to the sacrifice of praise Bill talked about.

Here is another unusual example of the mystery surrounding healing. A few years prior to Jenee's death, I was visiting the poor and taking food to the needy in our area for our local food bank. I purposefully had asked for the names of people who did not have a church already. I not only wanted to minister to the poor; I wanted to evangelize the lost. Since the median age of our church people was 23, I also specified that the age of the people on my list be under 55. I felt that people over 55 at that time (the mid-1980s) would not like the kind of church I was starting, especially the contemporary worship music.

One day two women from my church went with me to take food to the one of the people on my list. It was a young single mother of two daughters, ages five and seven. This young mother had never been married, and during our interview with her I discovered that she had been living with a man who had recently stolen her car, emptied her bank account and run off, leaving her destitute.

This young woman also had recently discovered that she had cancer. It had started in her brain, where the largest tumor was, and then it had metastasized into her lungs and several of her abdominal organs. She underwent chemotherapy for it, but the doctor told her she was terminal and had only a few weeks to live. He advised her to make a will and determine what would happen to her daughters when she died.

In the course of our interview, which we did with all the people we visited for the food bank, I also discovered that this woman not only did not have a church; she had only been to church once in her life, when she had been christened as a Lutheran. She did not know anything about the Christian faith and did not know how to pray.

After she finished telling me about her cancer and the terminal diagnosis, I asked, "Can I pray for you?"

"Yes," she replied.

I immediately put my hands on her head to begin to pray for her.

"What are you doing?" she asked me.

I responded, "You told me I could pray for you."

She responded, "Yes, but I didn't think you meant now. Pray for me when you get home or get to your church, not now."

"I believe God answers long-distance prayers," I told her, "but those are like Ph.D. prayers. I am in kindergarten in my learning about healing. Personally, I have never had someone healed when I prayed at a distance. I believe there is a much higher probability of you being healed if you let me pray for you here and now."

"Okay, go ahead then," she said. "Pray for me now."

Once again I placed my hands on her head and began to command the cancer to die. I prayed, "In the name of Jesus I command this cancer to die, and I command the tumor to shrink and die."

I had told her to let me know if she felt anything while I was praying, so she told me, "My head is getting hot!"

I responded, "That's good."

She responded, "You're weird!"

I kept praying for her, commanding the tumor to shrink, wither and die.

Then she said, "I feel electricity!"

I responded, "That's really good."

She responded, "And you're really weird!"

She continued to talk to me, which I believed would be detrimental to her healing. I thought she needed to be quiet, focus on the healing and tell me what she was feeling. But she continued to talk. While talking, she could not stay focused on what was happening so that it could cause her faith to grow. I was getting nervous that she was going to mess up the healing, but all of a sudden I had this impression from God: *Don't worry about it. This is on Me. Nothing she says or does is going to stop this healing.*

I repeated this scene with the young woman every two weeks for about three to four cycles before she called and told me that she did not need any more food or help since another man had moved in with her. Years later, I was again picking up food at the food pantry to take to the poor when I saw her.

"Sue, you're alive!" I yelled at her.

Taken by surprise, she came running over to me and said, "You embarrassed me! You're not supposed to yell at someone in public."

"I know," I responded, "but you're supposed to be dead! What happened?"

"You know I was supposed to die, but I was not getting any worse. After several weeks the doctor wanted to run more tests on me. When he did new MRIs and CAT scans, they couldn't find any cancer in my body. I always wondered if it had anything to do with you praying for me."

"Yes, it did," I told her. "Jesus healed you!"

Then I asked Sue if she would come to my church, where I was training a new ministry team to pray for the sick, and tell them her story. To my surprise, she agreed. When she came, she broke down and began to weep when she got to the part where the doctor had told her to make a will regarding her children's care.

I believe that God was pursuing this young lady through my encounters with her and through her healing. Maybe by now Sue has found her way into the Kingdom of God. I lost track of her several years ago, and I don't know what has happened to her since. But I have to admit that I did not have strong faith for Sue's healing, whereas I did have strong faith for Jenee's healing. Just the opposite happened, however, and I have to live with the mystery of it.

I have to admit that I cannot figure out why some people are healed and others are not. All I know is that Jesus did not say we should base our obedience on our understanding. We are called to believe and obey, even when we don't understand. And we are called to offer a sacrifice of praise. Those are the best answers I have found for how to handle unanswered prayer for healing.

22

A Solid Wall of Faith
for Healing

If I have the gift of prophecy and can fathom all
mysteries and all knowledge, and if I have a faith
that can move mountains, but do not have love, I
am nothing.

1 Corinthians 13:2

This second part of the book has been all about building a wall
of faith for a healing breakthrough. We have gathered a lot of
building materials together, so to speak, to build that wall. I
have provided you with many of the insights I have discovered
over more than three decades of healing ministry, and I have
presented you with numerous ways to create an atmosphere of
faith conducive to healing. To cement our wall together and
make it a really solid wall of faith for healing, let's briefly summarize some of the main things we have learned. While this
is not a complete list of everything we have discussed, I think
you will find it helpful.

One of the first things we learned is that there is a strong connection between faith and speaking out a word audibly. The word we speak can be a word of Scripture, or it can be a word God reveals to us about the situation we are praying for. If we receive a word in advance, we can speak out specifically what we will be praying for. This spoken word—not a sermon, but a specific insight from God on what to do—can change the faith level of the people, which in turn creates an atmosphere for healing breakthrough. A revelatory word often creates this kind of faith and may come in several different ways, such as a prophecy, a still, small voice, a word of knowledge or the quickening of a biblical text. We also learned that gifts of revelation from God create faith that in turn activates the gift of power—healing and miracles that are related closely to signs and wonders.

Another thing we learned is that an understanding of the "ways of God" helps create faith in us. Understanding His ways is a good foundation on which we can stand to experience an increase in our faith. But faith can also come as a gift. In fact, we learned that not all faith is the same; there are different types of faith. One type is the gift of faith that comes as grace; it is created by God and is actually His faith, or the measure of faith He supplies. Another type is the measure of faith we have, which can increase through our study and through our experiences of healing. Another type is the saving faith related to our conversion and salvation. Finally, there is the type of faith that deals with what we believe, specifically the content of the Christian Gospel and basic Christian doctrines, especially those in Hebrews 6:1–2.

We also studied the relationship between the *rhema* and *logos* words of God in their relationship to creating faith. Both words mean communication, although sometimes we contrast them by saying *logos* is the message itself and *rhema* is the communication of that message. Whatever way you define these two words, clearly the connection is very strong between hearing and receiving God's revelation and building faith.

In addition, we learned that it builds our faith to have direct experience with God healing people. For example, it has built my faith to experience the way God has healed so many people with metal in their bodies. Sometimes, seeing large numbers of people healed of one particular kind of problem can cause a gift of faith or a strong measure of faith to rise up in the person ministering healing.

We learned that the gift of faith—the faith *of* God that we talked about at some length—is almost always a key element in miracles. Healings, on the other hand, can be more related to our faith—faith *in* God. When the gift of God's faith comes to us, it removes all doubt and gives us great confidence. This is the mountain-moving faith *of* God instead of faith *in* God. (See Matthew 21:21; Mark 11:22–23; and 1 Corinthians 13:2.)

I also told you about my research for my doctoral thesis, in which I studied six variables to see whether they would increase the probability of someone being healed. My research showed that three of the variables I chose do show a measurable increase in the likelihood of someone receiving healing. If a person's theology of healing is good, the likelihood of healing increases. If the person has received prior training about healing, especially in regard to learning practical principles, the likelihood increases. And if the person has previous experience with healing, a healing is more likely.

The positive effect of the other three variables was not born out in my research, but that was due to the way I set up the study, which resulted in a confound. But my healing meetings and many years of ministry in this area do illustrate the positive effect of the remaining variables. Those variables are the person having an expectation of healing, words of knowledge being given and praying prayers of command rather than intercessory prayers. In effect, all six of the variables I studied increase the probability of healing.

By way of providing you with some practical applications, I went through my strategy for creating an atmosphere of faith for healing within a service. I gave you an order of service that I have found highly effective in my healing meetings. It included specific times for increasing the congregation's faith through teaching, through illustrations, through clearly explaining the ways of God in relationship to healing and through the use of testimonies about what Jesus is doing or has done. (I mentioned showing videos as one powerful way to release healing testimonies.) I also talked about why it is so important for the congregation to acknowledge what God is actually in the process of doing in a meeting. When you are ministering healing, you should instruct the congregation that those who are being healed should start acknowledging right away that God is doing something in them. (As I said, I direct them to stand and wave a hand when they feel anything, and to wave both hands when they are at least 80 percent better.) There are specific practices you can follow to help build that solid wall of faith for healing.

Finally, we looked at two of the not-so-thrilling aspects of healing ministry—dealing with people who "lose" their healing, and handling unanswered prayer for healing. It is always important to continue pressing in for healing, but different things can become hindrances. An environment of skepticism can cause a person to lose a healing. So can someone's refusal to make a lifestyle change that will address the issues behind his or her illness. (Going back to your old ways can bring a physical problem back even after you are healed.) Another hindrance can come in the form of afflicting spirits that may try to return after a healing. We must warn people that if returning symptoms of their illness manifest, it is important that they command the afflicting spirit to leave in Jesus' name to sustain the healing.

Knowing how to handle unanswered prayer for healing is vitally important because much about healing remains a mystery. There is so much that we still do not understand. Sometimes those people who you think are the best candidates for healing remain unhealed, while those who seem the most unlikely candidates are healed. Healing cannot be reduced to a science, nor is it mechanical. As much as I teach and use the Five-Step Prayer Model all over the world when I pray for people, healing ministry cannot be reduced to a formula. We have to accept the fact that the mystery remains, and, as Bill Johnson so aptly said, we need to offer a *sacrifice* of praise in the midst of it.

I hope you have found this book helpful. I hope it has given you a better understanding of the relationship between intimacy with God and revelation, between revelation and faith, and between faith and healing. Based on the reports of several thousand people who have taken some of our Global Awakening courses,[1] I believe that God has given me wisdom in regard to training people to minister in the gifts of the Spirit. I have done my best to share that wisdom with you in these pages, particularly as it applies to healing.

I wish you well as you seek to minister healing to others or find healing yourself. I hope all we talked about has encouraged you, and I want to pray this prayer for you:

Father, in Jesus' name I bless this reader. I pray for the gifts of the Holy Spirit to be released in him or her. I pray especially for a release of the gifts of words of knowledge, prophecy and faith. I pray for the gifts of healing and miracles to be released in his or her life and ministry. I pray for a fresh baptism in the Holy Spirit. I pray that

You would overwhelm this reader with peace, love and joy. I pray that he or she will experience the power of Your presence and the compassion of Your love. Come, Holy Spirit! Come, Holy Spirit! Fill this reader up! Fill this reader up! In the mighty name of Jesus, Amen.

NOTES

Introduction: How Healing Moved from Rare to Regular

1. The Five-Step Prayer Model I use and teach involves a specific process I go through with people who come to me for healing prayer. The five steps are 1) interview, 2) diagnosis and prayer selection, 3) prayer ministry (praying for effect), 4) stop and re-interview, and 5) post-prayer suggestions. While I have not covered the relational Five-Step Model in detail in this book, you can learn all about the process in *The Essential Guide to Healing* (Chosen, 2011), which Bill Johnson and I co-authored. There is also an *Essential Guide* curriculum kit available for deeper study, either in groups or individually.

2. Presently my ministry, Global Awakening, offers some separate four-day schools that include six teachings per day. The *Kingdom Foundations* school deals with the foundations for healing. The *Empowered* school deals with more lessons on physical healing, but includes an additional five teachings on deliverance, and also teachings on the difference between New Age healing modalities and Christian healing. There are also lectures that repudiate cessationism (the belief that the gifts of healing, working of miracles, prophecy, tongues and interpretation of tongues have ceased), and liberalism (a theological position that denies the supernatural). The *Healing: Spiritual and Medical Perspectives* school was designed to deal specifically with what the medical field is learning about healing and how this fits with what the Church is learning. The *Foundations of Faith* school focuses especially on the relationship of faith to healing, and it analyzes the validity and challenges of the Faith Cure movement and the Word of Faith movement. Each school offers teachings on words of knowledge, the Five-Step Prayer Model and impartation, because these three foundational things are so key to helping people experience a breakthrough in healing.

3. For more information on raising the dead, see the course offered by the Wagner Leadership Institute of Global Awakening, "Missions 101—Raising the Dead," https://globalawakening.com/schools/wli/wli-course-information.

4. For more information on what has taken place in Mozambique, see Donald R. Kantel, "Downstream from Toronto: The 'Toronto Blessing' Revival & Iris Ministries in Mozambique" (D.Min. diss., Regent Divinity School, 2007).

5. This is a theme in two books by Dr. Jon Mark Ruthven, *On the Cessation of the Charismata: The Protestant Polemic on Post-biblical Miracles* (Word & Spirit Press, 2011), and *What's Wrong with Protestant Theology? Tradition vs. Biblical Emphasis* (Word & Spirit Press, 2013).

Chapter 1: Paul's Thorn in the Flesh

1. For more on this idea of Paul's thorn in the flesh representing adversaries, see F. F. Bosworth's *Christ the Healer* (Chosen, 2008), Michael Brown's *Israel's Divine Healer* (Zondervan, 1995), and David Harrell Jr.'s *All Things Are Possible: The Healing and Charismatic Revivals in Modern America* (Indiana University Press, 1979).

Chapter 2: An Overemphasis on Sovereignty

1. Gregory Boyd, *God at War: The Bible and Spiritual Conflict* (Downers Grove, Ill.: InterVarsity, 1997), 18–22.

2. Ibid., 238–68.

3. Ibid., 269–93.

4. Morton Kelsey, *Healing and Christianity* (San Francisco: Harper & Row, reprinted Augsburg, 1973, 1995), 15–16.

5. Ibid., 12.

6. Ibid., 18.

7. For more on Arminianism, see http://christianheritagefellowship.com/the-origin-of-arminian-theology/.

8. The *Remonstrance* document particularly challenged Calvin's TULIP theology. TULIP stands for Total depravity, Unconditional election, Limited atonement, Irresistible grace and Perseverance of the saints. In TULIP, the *Remonstrance* document disagreed with ULI and had concerns about P.

9. For more on Open Theism, see http://opentheism.info/, cf. http://en.wikipedia.org/wiki/Open_theism. See also https://carm.org/what-is-open-theism, which is actually an article against Open Theism, but the "Books and Websites Consulted" list at the end of the article, which lists both "For Open Theism" and "Against Open Theism" materials, would be most helpful for those wanting to learn more about this debate. You can find another good source for pro and con materials at http://www.theopedia.com/Open_theism (although the article itself is negative regarding Open Theism).

10. For more on Process Theology, see http://www.processandfaith.org.

Chapter 3: The Big Lie about Faith

1. See chapters 3 and 4 of MacMullen's *Christianizing the Roman Empire* (Yale University Press, 1984). See also Adolf Harnack's *The Mission and Expansion of Christianity in the First Three Centuries*, available through the Christian Classics Ethereal Library at http:www.ccel.org/ccel/harnack/mission.html.

2. In particular, refer to chapters 1, 6–10, 11 and 15 of *Supernatural Missions* for more on the missiological impact of signs, wonders, healings and deliverances.

3. This statement is based on a conversation I had with a missionary from the Sinai Peninsula who had come from a gathering of all the missionaries on the Peninsula, almost all of whom were evangelical, not Pentecostal or charismatic. What they discovered was that none of them had ever led a Muslim to the Lord unless the person had first seen a miracle or healing, or had had a dream about Jesus or a vision of Him. Some of these missionaries had been working there for as many as 38 years. Upon this discovery, they sent a delegation to talk to Dr. Jack Deere to see if he would come and teach them. Deere suggested that they meet with Bill Johnson or me instead. Rolland and Heidi Baker in Mozambique's two most Muslim provinces had a similar experience with the Makua tribe. An evangelical missionary group had tried to reach this people group of 18 million unsuccessfully for 25 years. The Bakers were able to help reach the tribe due to signs and wonders, along with tangibly demonstrating their love in meeting the tribe members' social needs.

Chapter 8: A Deistic or Liberal Worldview

1. Jon Ruthven, *What's Wrong With Protestant Theology? Tradition vs. Biblical Emphasis* (Tulsa: Word & Spirit Press, 2013), 153.

Chapter 9: "Sickness Is My Cross to Bear"

1. Francis MacNutt, *Healing* (Notre Dame: Ave Maria Press, 1974), 31–32.

Chapter 10: Mistaking Emotionalism for Faith

1. Jon Ruthven, *What's Wrong With Protestant Theology? Tradition vs. Biblical Emphasis* (Tulsa: Word & Spirit Press, 2013), 212.

2. For more on this story, see my book *There Is More! The Secret to Experiencing God's Power to Change Your Life* (Chosen, 2013), 64–66.

3. For more on Bob's story, see my book *Baptism in the Holy Spirit* (Global Awakening, 2009), 49–50.

4. Saint Augustine, *The Confessions of St. Augustine*, trans. Rex Warner (New York: New American Library/Mentor-Omega Books, 1963), 173.

5. Ibid., 173–74.

6. Ibid., 182.

7. Ibid.

8. Ibid., 183.

9. Ibid.

10. John J. O'Meara, *The Young Augustine: The Growth of St. Augustine's Mind Up to His Conversion* (London: Longmans, Green and Co., 1954), 179.

11. I recorded my fillings or baptisms in the Holy Spirit in some of my books. For more detail, see *Lighting Fires* (Global Awakening, 1998), 51, 53–54, 77–78, and *There Is More! The Secret to Experiencing God's Power to Change Your Life* (Chosen, 2013), 35–36. (I highly recommend reading *There Is More!* for great insight into the

whole doctrine of impartation or the laying on of hands, found in Hebrews 6:1–2.) For the most explicit detail about my experiences of being filled or baptized in the Holy Spirit, see my book *Baptism in the Holy Spirit* (Global Awakening, 2009).

Chapter 11: Overreaction to the "Word of Faith" Position

1. Jon Ruthven, *What's Wrong with Protestant Theology? Tradition vs. Biblical Emphasis* (Tulsa: Word & Spirit Press, 2013), 239.

2. Joe McIntyre, *E. W. Kenyon and His Message of Faith: The True Story* (Bothell, Wash.: Empowering Grace Ministries, 2010), 54–59.

3. Ibid., 18–19.

4. Herbert Benson, *Timeless Healing: The Power and Biology of Belief* (New York: Simon & Schuster Fireside Edition, 1997), 273–74.

5. For a greater understanding of the diverse teachings on healing, see my book *The Healing River and Its Contributing Streams* (Global Awakening, 2013).

Chapter 13: Back to Seminary at 59

1. Dr. Park encouraged me to publish my thesis, and I am doing so for those readers who would like to study my thesis material in more depth. It will come out under the title *Authority to Heal* (Destiny Image, 2017).

Chapter 14: Relating Spoken Words to Faith

1. Visit https://www.youtube.com/watch?v=mukaOJJJbtQ&feature=youtu .be to see video testimonies of some of these healings.

2. Two more Scriptures come to mind that would be applicable to this discussion, although I did not use them in my sermons about faith, healing and declaration. The first is Matthew 21:21, in which Jesus said, "Truly I tell you, if you have faith and do not doubt, not only can you do what was done to the fig tree, but also you can say to this mountain, 'Go, throw yourself into the sea,' and it will be done." The second is Mark 11:22–23, in which He said, "Have faith in God. Truly I tell you, if anyone says to this mountain, 'Go, throw yourself into the sea,' and does not doubt in their heart but believes that what they say will happen, it will be done for them."

3. Here is scriptural support for the statement that in the Old Testament the *testimony* consisted of God's mighty deeds among the people (all taken from the NRSV):

"Remember the *wonderful works* he has done, his *miracles*" (1 Chronicles 16:12, emphasis added).

"One generation shall laud your *works* to another, and shall declare your *mighty acts*. . . . all your faithful shall bless you. They shall speak of the glory of your kingdom, and tell of your *power*, to make known to all people your *mighty deeds*" (Psalm 145:4, 10–12, emphasis added).

"I will come praising the *mighty deeds* of the Lord GOD, I will praise your righteousness, yours alone. O God, from my youth you have taught me, and I still proclaim your *wondrous deeds*. So even to old age and gray hairs, O God, do not forsake me, until I proclaim your might to all the generations to come. Your *power* and your righteousness, O God, reach the high heavens. You who have done *great things*, O God, who is like you?" (Psalm 71:16–19, emphasis added).

"We will not hide them from their children; we will tell to the coming generation the *glorious deeds* of the LORD, and his *might*, and the *wonders* that he has done. He established a decree in Jacob, and appointed a law in Israel, which he commanded our ancestors to teach to their children; that the next generation might know them, the children yet unborn, and rise up and tell them to their children, *so that they should set their hope in God, and not forget the works* of God . . . and that they should not be like their ancestors . . . whose spirit was not faithful to God . . . *They forgot what he had done, and the miracles that he had shown them*" (Psalm 78:4–11, emphasis added).

"I will meditate on *all your work*, and muse on your *mighty deeds*. Your way, O God, is holy. What god is so great as our God? You are the God who *works wonders*; you have displayed *your might* among the peoples. With your *strong arm* you redeemed your people" (Psalm 77:12–15, emphasis added).

"O give thanks to the LORD, call on his name, make known his *deeds* among the peoples. Sing to him, sing praises to him; tell of *all his wonderful works*. Glory in his holy name; let the hearts of those who seek the LORD rejoice. Seek the LORD and *his strength*; seek his presence continually. Remember the *wonderful works* he has done, *his miracles*" (Psalm 105:1–5, emphasis added).

4. Bill Johnson has stated this many times in Global Awakening's Schools of Healing and Impartation over the past nine years.

5. These healing ministers include Heidi Baker, Bill Johnson, James Maloney, Omar Cabrera, Carlos Annacondia, Leif Hetland, Henry Madava, Cal Pierce, Ian Andrews, Jim and Ramona Rickard, James Maloney and Todd White.

6. You can view video testimony of these healings at http://www.youtube.com/watch?v=BXM58ji-5kI&feature=youtu.be. The man who testified in the video that he had a metal rod implanted in his right arm also told me during the meeting that he had seventeen screws in that arm.

Chapter 15: Receiving Revelation

1. You can view *God Squad* at http://www.youtube.com/watch?v=wFn4OV GnVMI and http://www.youtube.com/watch?v=yPfgs1tW67w.

2. Saint Augustine, *The Confessions of St. Augustine,* trans. Rex Warner (New York: New American Library/Mentor-Omega Books, 1963), 174–183.

Chapter 16: Faith and the Ways of God

1. One of Global Awakening's associate evangelists, Paul Martini, has the best teaching I have ever heard on the power of peace. You can order it as a DVD at http://globalawakeningstore.com/The-Power-of-Peace-DVD.html.

2. Among these are Young's Literal Translation, the Douay-Rheims Bible, the Bible in Basic English, the Geneva Bible and the German Neue Luther Bibel (New Lutheran Bible).

3. For more on this concept of faith as a gift, see Dr. Price's book *The Real Faith* in its original version (Revival Library Reprints, unabridged, 1940).

4. I wrote my doctoral thesis on this subject: "A Study of the Effects of Christian Prayer on Pain or Mobility Restrictions from Surgeries Involving Implanted Materials" (Doctor of Ministry Thesis: United Theological Seminary: Dayton, Ohio, 2013).

Chapter 17: Different Types of Faith

1. Herbert Benson, *Timeless Healing: The Power and Biology of Belief* (New York: Simon & Schuster Fireside Edition, 1997), 196–97, 206.

2. See Charles Price's *The Real Faith* (Revival Library Reprints, unabridged, 1940). This is the emphasis throughout his entire book. As I talked about in chapter 16, faith that moves mountains is not our faith, but comes as a gift from God and is actually the faith *of* God rather than faith *in* God. See also the section titled "Pentecostal Studies for Verification of Healings and Miracles" in my doctoral thesis, "A Study of the Effects of Christian Prayer on Pain or Mobility Restrictions from Surgeries Involving Implanted Materials" (Doctor of Ministry Thesis: United Theological Seminary: Dayton, Ohio, 2013).

3. *Theological Dictionary of the New Testament (TDNT)*, s.v. "pistis." It is interesting not only to consider what Bultmann covers in this article on faith, but also to note what he does not mention or develop. He offers no discussion of the relationship between faith and healing, faith and miracles, faith and signs and wonders, or faith and power. For more on this, see also Jon Ruthven, *What's Wrong with Protestant Theology? Tradition vs. Biblical Emphasis* (Tulsa: Word & Spirit Press, 2013), 127–59.

4. See Ruthven's *What's Wrong with Protestant Theology?* and also his *On the Cessation of the Charismata* (Word & Spirit Press, 2011). See also Greig's *The Kingdom and the Power: Are Healing and the Spiritual Gifts Used by Jesus and the Early Church Meant for the Church Today?* (Ventura, Calif.: Regal, 1993), 149–61.

5. See Ruthven, *What's Wrong*, especially chapters 7–10.

6. For help in learning how to recognize God's communications to us, see the book I co-authored with Bill Johnson, *The Essential Guide to Healing* (Chosen, 2011). Better yet, study *The Essential Guide* in detail by going through the curriculum we put together for it (eight video teachings, a workbook and a leader's guide are available from Chosen, either separately or in a kit. See also my book *Words of Knowledge* (Global Awakening, 2011).

7. *Rhema* is the word used for faith in Romans 10:8 (NIV1984), "But what does it say? 'The word is near you; it is in your mouth and in your heart,' that is, the word of faith we are proclaiming."

8. *TDNT*, s.v. "logos."

9. The Greek word *rhema* exclusively denotes the spoken word. In Walter Bauer's standard New Testament Greek-English lexicon, *rhema* denotes that which is said, a saying, a statement, speech, a prophecy, a declaration, a command, an order, a threat, a proclamation or [spoken] teaching. The Greek word *logos* has a broader semantic range and can denote both the written word, including Scripture, and the spoken word. *Logos* can denote a literary work, books, a treatise, a book of Scripture or a written ledger of income and expenses. It can also denote an oral utterance, a statement, a prophecy, a report or a story. From W. Bauer and F. W. Gingrich, *Greek-English Lexicon of the New Testament and Other Early Christian Literature*, 3rd ed., ed. W. F. Arndt and F. W. Danker (Chicago: University of Chicago Press, 2001), 920–21.

10. *Third Wave* is the term coined by Dr. C. Peter Wagner for the movement made up primarily of evangelicals who left cessationism and believed in continuationism of the gifts of the Holy Spirit, but who would not identify with the two classic pillars of Pentecostal theology—the doctrine of subsequence and the doctrine of tongues being the necessary and initial evidence of the baptism in the Holy Spirit. Most within the Third Wave Movement would grant that the baptism in the Holy Spirit most often occurred subsequent to salvation, but would not believe tongues are necessary or always initial evidence of being baptized in the Holy Spirit.

11. Jim B. McClure, *Grace Revisited* (Geelong, Australia: Trailblazer, 2010), 61.

12. See chapter 5 of my doctoral thesis, "Reflection, Summary, and Conclusion," pages 232–81 (and in particular 254–77). My thesis is "A Study of the Effects of Christian Prayer on Pain or Mobility Restrictions from Surgeries Involving Implanted Materials" (Doctor of Ministry Thesis: United Theological Seminary: Dayton, Ohio, 2013).

13. Other Scriptures that refer to a saving type of faith are these: "For in the gospel a righteousness from God is revealed, a righteousness that is by faith from first to last, just as it is written: 'The righteous will live by faith'" (Romans 1:17 NIV1984). "This righteousness from God comes through faith in Jesus Christ to all who believe" (Romans 3:22 NIV1984). "What then shall we say? That the Gentiles, who did not pursue righteousness, have obtained it, a righteousness that is by faith . . ." (Romans 9:30 NIV1984). See also Romans 3:25–30; 4:5, 9, 16–20. (That last section of Romans 4 also fits with faith for the miraculous since it was impossible for Abraham and Sarah to conceive naturally.)

14. Note that this verse is important in a salvation context, but also in regard to healing and miracles.

15. Note that the measure of faith this passage refers to does not just deal with salvation. The context is the gift of prophecy. This principle of the gifts operating by faith, in proportion to one's faith, should apply to the other gifts as well, for that is the context. The proportion of faith, or measure of faith, someone has can increase by another gift of revelation (a *rhema* word of God) that reveals the will of God in that situation. This means a person can move from a measure of his or her faith to the mountain-moving faith of God that is a gift.

Chapter 18: The Probability of Healing

1. Iris Ministries, now called Iris Global, is the missionary organization started by Heidi and Rolland Baker in 1980. Iris now has 35 bases in about 20 nations. You can find out more at https://www.irisglobal.org.

2. Charles Price, *The Real Faith: Original Pentecostal Classics Editions*, 2nd ed. (EM Publications: Wichita, Kansas, 2008), 24–26.

3. Ibid., 27.

4. Ibid., 30.

5. See Francis MacNutt, *Healing* (Notre Dame: Ave Maria Press, 1974), 113–14.

6. Price, *Real Faith*, 33.

7. Ibid., 35.

Chapter 20: Contending for Breakthrough

1. Randy Clark and Craig Miller, *Finding Victory When Healing Doesn't Happen: Breaking Through with Healing Prayer* (Mechanicsburg, Penn.: Apostolic Network of Global Awakening, 2015), 105–6.

Chapter 22: A Solid Wall of Faith for Healing

1. People in both Global Awakening's online certification programs have written us reviews about how helpful our classes have been in breaking them into a new realm of discipleship, healing. You can find information on the Christian Healing Certification Program (CHCP) at www.healingcertification.com and on the Christian Prophetic Certification Program (CPCP) at www.prophetic certification.com. Jon Ruthven, professor emeritus of Regent University Divinity School, also wrote a fantastic review of Global Awakening in his latest book, *What's Wrong with Protestant Theology?* (Word & Spirit Press, 2013). He told his readers, "See the website for Randy Clark's ministry, Global Awakening, which, in my opinion is about the most sane, informed, balanced, biblical, humble, and spiritually powerful Christian organization out there: www.globalawakening.com. This is a great place to be mentored and trained for effective, biblical ministry." I encourage you to join me in learning more about healing by enrolling in one of our multiple healing schools, either in person or online, or by attending one of our conferences. You can also accompany us on an international ministry trip. Visit the Global Awakening website for details.

Index

activation/impartation, 22, 207n2
afflicting spirits
  command of in Jesus' name, 178–79,
    204
  and the migration of pain, 131–34
allegorical method, 65
  and the school of Alexandria, 65
amen
  "amen" to the glory of God, 106
  speaking the amen, 115–16
Andrews, Ian, 211n5
angels, 109, 159
Annacondia, Carlos, 211n5
apostles, the
  need for the continued ministry of
    apostles, 61
  as not primarily writers of Scripture, 61
  as strategic church planters, 61
Aquinas, Thomas, 39
Arminianism, 39
Augustine, 39
  conversion of, 74, 123–24
Authority to Heal (R. Clark), 210n1
  (chap. 13)

Baker, Heidi, 20, 59, 209n3 (chap. 7),
    211n5, 214n1 (chap. 18)
  baptism of in the Holy Spirit, 72
Baker, Rolland, 20, 59, 72, 209n3 (chap. 7),
    214n1 (chap. 18)

Balassi, Bob, baptism of in the Holy
    Spirit, 73
baptism in the Holy Spirit, 72–73
  and Bob Balassi, 73
  and Heidi Baker, 72
  and Randy Clark, 72
Baptism in the Holy Spirit (R. Clark),
    209n3 (chap. 10), 210n11
Baptists
  and cessationism, 183
  understanding of words of knowledge,
    117
Bartimaeus, as an illustration of how a
    word of knowledge works, 166
  the throwing of his cloak to the ground
    as a sign of faith, 166
Benson, Herbert, 143, 144
  on "cognitive restructuring," 82–83
Berry, Timothy, 59
Big Lie about faith, the, 30, 41–46, 86
  and hermeneutical issues, 42–44
  and the historical issue, 45
  and the liberal pastor or scholar, 44
  and the missiological issue, 45–46
  reliance on John 4:48 and John 20:29, 42
blueprint worldview, 30, 35–40, 86
  overemphasis of on God's sovereignty,
    37, 40
  as a replacement for the warfare world-
    view, 36

Book of Common Prayer, Office of the Visitation of the Sick, 37, 38
Bosworth, F. F., 34, 164, 208n1 (chap. 1)
Boyd, Gregory, 36
Branham, William, 159, 164
Brown, Michael, 34, 208n1 (chap. 1)
Bultmann, Rudolf, 147, 212n3 (chap. 17)
Byrne, Annie, 59

Cabrera, Omar, 108–9, 113, 159, 164, 211n5
Calvin, John, 39
  TULIP theology of, 208n8
cessationism, 30, 59–62, 64, 87–88
  basis of, 60
  use of 1 Corinthians 13:8–10, 61
charismata. *See* spiritual gifts
Christ the Healer (Bosworth), 208n1 (chap. 1)
Christian Science, 78
Christianizing the Roman Empire (MacMullen), 208n1 (chap. 3)
Clark, DeAnne, 31, 119, 195
  healing of, 167–68
Clark, Josh, 96
Clark, Randy, 45, 60, 179, 209nn2–3 (chap. 10), 209–10n11, 210n5, 212n6
  baptism of in the Holy Spirit, 75
  call of into ministry, 184
  "clear the rubble" message of, 29
  college education of, 184
  conversion of, 74–75
  doctoral studies at United Theological Seminary, 97–100
  and Grandma Ray's healing, 181, 182, 183
  and Grandpa Ray's death, 181–83
  healing of his back, 94–97
  healing in his first pastorate, 186–89
  healing of his life-threatening injuries, 183–84
  and Immogene's healing, 181, 182, 183
  initial attempts to get his doctorate, 94–97
  life verses of (2 Corinthians 1:18–20; 2 Corinthians 4:13; Revelation 19:10), 103–8
  master's studies of, 65, 98, 184–86
  measure of faith of when it comes to praying for healing, 122, 138–41, 142

reasons for his return to seminary at age 59, 93–94
  reception of a gift of faith, 119–20
  thesis research of, 155–58, 202–3
  visits of to the Baptist church in Mauá, Brazil, 101–3
Confessions of Saint Augustine, The, 74
Cook, Blaine, 21, 71, 109, 119

Deere, Jack, 209n3 (chap. 7)
deism, 30, 64–65, 88
demons, 36, 37
"Downstream from Toronto: The 'Toronto Blessing' Revival & Iris Ministries in Mozambique" (Kantel), 208n4
Duncan, Billy, 186–87

E. W. Kenyon and His Message of Faith: The True Story (McIntyre), 78
Emerson College, 78–79
emotions, proper place for, 71–75
Enlightenment, the, 65
Essential Guide curriculum kit, 207n1
Essential Guide to Healing, The (R. Clark and B. Johnson), 60, 207n1, 212n6
Essential Guide to the Holy Spirit, The: God's Miraculous Gifts at Work Today (R. Clark), 60
evangelicalism, 64
expecting not enough (underrealized eschatology), 30, 57–58, 87
expecting too much (overrealized eschatology), 57

faith, 144–47
  creating an atmosphere of, 146
  degrees of, 150–51
  faith *in* God, 136, 202
  and healing, 121
  meanings of the word *faith* in Scripture, 150
  the measure of faith, 122, 141–42, 152, 201, 213n15
  mistaking emotionalism for faith, 30, 70–75, 88
  and mystery, 146
  naturalistic ("mind over matter") faith, 144
  rhema, logos and faith, 147–48, 201–2
  saving faith, 152–54, 161, 201, 213n13
  seeing someone's faith, 127

See also faith *of* God; faith and the ways of God

faith *of* God, 135–38, 144, 158–61, 202

Bible translations using "faith *of* God" rather than "faith *in* God," 212n2

as faith that can "move mountains," 137, 144, 158, 213n15

as a gift, 110, 119–20, 201, 213n5

as God-infused, 151–52

as a situational gift of grace, 159, 161–64

Faith Cure movement, 78

faith and the ways of God, 27, 115, 115–16, 125–27, 145–46, 201

and the celebration of God's presence, 130–31

faith and the excellent way, 134

and knowing God, 145

leveling up in faith, 141–42

manifestations of the Holy Spirit, 125–30

the migration of a manifestation, 131–34

Moses' prayer that God would teach him His ways, 27, 145

no more playing it safe, 138–41

and the presence of God, 145

and seeing God's glory, 145

types of faith Scripture refers to, 154

Fall, the, 189

false humility, 51–56, 87

as the opposite of hype, 51–52

Finding Victory When Healing Doesn't Happen (Miller), 179

Five-Step Prayer Model, 22, 176, 204, 207n1, 207n3

the five steps of, 207n1

fruit

fruit of doing, 53

fruit of the Spirit, 53

fundamentalism, 64

Galloway, Jamie, 122

Global Awakening, 22, 207n2, 214n1 (chap. 22)

Christian Healing Certification Program (CHCP) of, 214n1 (chap. 22)

Christian Prophetic Certification Program (CPCP) of, 214n1 (chap. 22)

Empowered school of, 207n2

Faith and Healing school of, 84

Foundations of Faith school of, 207n2

Healing: Spiritual and Medical Perspectives school of, 207n2

Kingdom Foundations school of, 207n2

God

bringing God glory, 52–53

glory of, 145

intentionality of, 114–15, 115

sovereignty of and salvation, 25–26

See also faith and the ways of God; grace, of God

God Squad, 123, 211n1 (chap. 15)

Gospel, the, 26

and healing, 26–27

grace, of God, 27, 134, 151, 201

and "gracelets," 27, 134, 144, 152

Grace Revisited (McClure), 151

Great Commission, 191

Greig, Gary, 94, 99, 147

Hagin, Kenneth, 79

Hanfere, Paulos, 59, 60

Harnack, Adolf, 208n1 (chap. 3)

Harrell, David, Jr., 208n1 (chap. 1)

Hart, Will, 59, 122

Harvey, Van A., 65

healing, 144

and the advancement of the Kingdom of God, 25–26

and faith *in* God, 144

and the faith of the person who is healing, 24

and God's glorifying of His name, 52

God's speeding up of healings, 20

healing as normative, 21, 22–23, 57–58, 87

hindrances to healing prayer, 175

inconsistent healings, 24–25

and mystery, 26, 27, 146

natural healings, 21

New Age healing modalities, 99

occurrence of at different times, 23

as part of the Gospel, 27–28

relation of to faith, 121

and resting in the promise, 180

of stroke victims, 19–20

supernatural healings, 21

the variety of results, 174–75

See also healing, critics of, why they are incorrect; healing, getting healed and staying healed; healing, handling unanswered prayer for; healing, "loss" of/hindrances to

healing, critics of, why they are incorrect
  healing is not dependent on the person
    who prays, 23–24
  the internal body-mind-spirit mecha-
    nism cannot be used, 23
  naturalistic and placebo explanations
    are untenable, 23
healing, foundation for. *See* activation/
    impartation; Five-Step Prayer Model;
    words of knowledge
healing, getting healed and staying
    healed, 178–80
  and building each other up, 179–80
  command in Jesus' name of afflicting
    spirits, 178–79, 204
  and focusing on what God has done,
    178–79
  and levels of expectation, 178
  and reading Scripture, 178
healing, handling unanswered prayer for,
    189–90, 204
  and the continual reception of prayer,
    191
  and mystery, 189, 193–94
  and the sacrifice of praise, 193–94,
    196, 199
  stories of unanswered healing, 190–99
healing, "loss" of. *See* healing, hin-
    drances to
healing, hindrances to, 175, 203–4
  emotional and spiritual afflictions, 177,
    203–4
  fear, 177
  lack of support, 177
  lifestyle issues, 176–77, 203
  and the need for encouragement, 177–78
  skepticism, 203
  worry, 175–76
healing, obstacles to. *See* Big Lie about
    faith, the; blueprint worldview; cessa-
    tionism; deism; expecting not enough
    (underrealized eschatology); false
    humility; hype; liberalism; mistaking
    emotionalism for faith; overreaction
    to the Word of Faith position; Paul's
    thorn in the flesh; "sickness is my
    cross to bear"
Healing (MacNutt), 67–68, 163, 187
Healing and Christianity (Morton), 37–39
*Healing River and Its Contributing
    Streams, The* (R. Clark), 210n5

healing services, 203
  and the 80 percent indicator, 112, 168,
    169, 170–71, 172, 203
  effective order of, 166–69, 203
  and "live" healing testimonies, 172
  questions to ask people giving healing
    testimonies, 172
  and testimony videos, 171–72, 203
  and those being prayed for, 173
  and those ministering healing, 173
Hebrews, book of, on signs and wonders,
    45
Hetlund, Leif, 59, 211n5
Historian and the Believer, The (Harvey),
    65
historical-critical method, 65
  basis of, 65–66
  and the Enlightenment, 65
  and Newtonian physics, 65
historical-grammatical method, 65
  and the school of Antioch, 65
Holiness movement, 78
Holy Spirit
  and conviction, 123
  manifestations of, 127–30
  and the reading of Scripture, 123
Howard-Browne, Rodney, 83
hype, 30, 47–50, 86–87
  definition of, 48
  the *do* list for moving naturally in the
    supernatural, 49–50
  the *don't* list for moving naturally in
    the supernatural, 49
  and loss of integrity, 48
  and revving people up emotionally, 48,
    70–71
  and speaking "evangelastically," 48–49

India, conversions and healings in, 26
interpretation of tongues, 121–22
Iris Ministries, 214n1 (chap. 18)
Israel's Divine Healer (Brown), 208n1
    (chap. 1)

Jesus
  command of afflicting spirits by,
    178–79, 204
  connecting of words to the release of
    the energy of heaven, 28
  on degrees of faith, 150–51
  on the fruit of doing, 53

high priestly prayer of, 53
as poor, not wealthy, 78
as Prophet, 54
seven signs of in the gospel of John,
    42–43, 44, 53–55
testimony of, 107–8
understanding of the importance of
    signs and wonders to faith, 43
Upper Room discourse of, 52–53, 148–50
and the woman at the well, 123
See also Messiah, the
Jesus movement, 17
John, gospel of, Jesus' seven signs in,
    42–43, 44, 53–55
Johnson, Bill, 59, 60, 78, 138, 140, 164,
    211nn4–5, 212n6
and his father's death, 192–94
measure of faith of in prayers for heal-
    ing, 122
on prophecy, 108
on testimony, 108
Johnson, Melvin Earl, 192–94
Jones, Tom, 84, 98–99
Judaisers, 33
as "super apostles," 33

Kantel, Donald R., 208n4
Kenyon, E. W., 78–79
opposition of to New Thought, 78
Kesley, Morton, 37–39
King, Paul, 80, 84

Lazarus, 54–55, 68–69
liberalism, 30, 64, 88
and the historical-critical method, 65
Lighting Fires (R. Clark), 209n11
logos, 148, 213n9
    logos, rhema and faith, 147–48

MacMullen, Ramsay, 45, 208n1 (chap. 3)
MacNutt, Francis, 67–68, 187
on prayer, 162–63
Madava, Henry, 59, 211n5
Maloney, James, 59, 138, 211n5
Martini, Paul, 59, 211n1 (chap. 16)
McClure, Jim, 151
McIntyre, Joe, 78, 79, 84
Messiah, the
as both Prophet and King, 54
as a King, 54
as a Prophet, 54

metanoia, 86
Metcalf, Johnny, 18–19
*Midas Touch, The: A Balanced Approach
    to Biblical Prosperity* (Hagin), 79
Miller, Craig, 179
miracles, 21, 144
as an expression of the Gospel of the
    Kingdom, 60
and the faith *of* God, 144
and God's glorifying of His name, 52
*Mission and Expansion of Christianity
    in the First Three Centuries, The*
    (Harnack), 208n1 (chap. 3)
Montanism, 62
Montanus, 62
Moses, prayer of, 27, 145
Mozambique
conversions and church growth in, 24,
    159–60
raising of the dead in, 24, 159–60
Muslims, conversion of to Christianity,
    24, 46, 209n3

New Covenant, 147
New Thought, 78, 78–79

O'Connor, Luther, 99
O'Meara, John J., 74
*On the Cessation of the Charismata: The
    Protestant Polemic on Post-biblical
    Miracles* (Ruthven), 208n5
*Only Believe: Examining the Origin and
    Development of Classic and Con-
    temporary Word of Faith Theologies*
    (King), 80, 84
Open Theism, 39–40, 208n9
Orthodox Churches, belief of in heal-
    ing, 36

Park, Andrew Sung, 97–98, 99, 210n1
    (chap. 13)
Paul
on "amen" to the glory of God, 106
on the fruit of the Spirit, 53
on the measure of faith, 152
on the promises of God as "Yes" in
    Christ, 105–6
on saving faith, 153–54, 213n13
on signs and wonders, 44–45
on speaking with the spirit of faith,
    106–7

on spiritual gifts, 135
See also Paul's thorn in the flesh
Paul's thorn in the flesh, 30, 31–34, 86
faulty logic behind the teaching of, 31–32
references to thorns in the Old Testament, 33–34
the thorn as given to Paul to keep him from becoming conceited, 33
the thorn as a person, fallen angel or demon, 33
Pentecostal theology, two classic pillars of, 213n10
Peter, seeing the faith of the man at the Gate Beautiful, 127
physics, Newtonian, 65
Pierce, Cal, 211n5
power evangelism, 122–23
Price, Charles, 137–38, 212n3 (chap. 16), 212n2 (chap. 17)
on belief, 162
on the connection between faith and belief, 163
on faith that creates miracles, 138
on faith as a gift from God, 162
on faith as a grace, 161–62
healing of at an Aimee Semple McPherson meeting, 137, 161
on prayer, 162–63
pride. *See* false humility
Process Theology, 40, 208n10
prophecy, 108, 115, 148
the testimony of Jesus as the spirit of prophecy, 107–8
Psychology, Religion, and Healing (Weatherhead), 144

raising of the dead, 20–21
Jesus' raising of Lazarus, 68–69
in Mozambique, 24, 159–60
Real Faith, The (Price), 137–38, 212n3 (chap. 16)
Remonstrance, 39
and TULIP, 208n8
revelation
receiving revelation, 117–24
and relationship, 148–50
revelatory gifts, 134, 201
gifts of power, 108, 109, 201
gifts of revelation, 108, 109, 134, 201
(*see also* words of knowledge)

gifts of speech, 109, 201 (*see also* interpretation of tongues; prophecy; tongues)
as "gracelets," 134
relationship between, 108–11
revelatory words, terms for
"inspiration from God," 148
"the Lord led me," 148
"the Lord told me," 148
"words from God," 148
See also prophecy; words of knowledge
rhema, 148, 212n7, 213n9
rhema, logos and faith, 147–48
Rhema Bible Church, 83
Rickard, Jim and Ramona, 211n5
Rocha, Ed, 59
Rogawski, Ralph, 68
Roman Catholic Church, Last Rites of, 36
Ruthven, Jon, 44, 63, 70, 76, 94, 97, 99, 147, 208n5, 212n3 (chap. 17), 214n1 (chap. 22)

salvation, and God's sovereignty, 26–27
Satan, 36, 37, 189
School of Healing and Impartation, 24
"sickness is my cross to bear," 30, 67–69, 88
lack of New Testament passages concerning, 68–69
as rooted in popular Catholic thought, 68
signs and wonders
in the book of Hebrews, 45
in the entirety of Scripture, 44
and God's glorifying of His name, 52
in the gospel of John, 42–43, 44
Paul on, 44–45
Smith, Hannah Whitall, 78
Smith, Ray, 96–97
soteriology, and God's salvation, 26–27
spiritual gifts, 135
desire for, 135
exercise of with love as our motivation, 135
as "gracelets," 26
and "the Lord's hand," 62
and the possibility for all believers to experience them, 62
See also revelatory gifts

"Study of the Effects of Christian Prayer on Pain or Mobility Restrictions from Surgeries Involving Implanted Materials, A" (R. Clark), 212n4 (chap. 16)
"Pentecostal Studies for Verification of Healings and Miracles" section in, 212n2 (chap. 17)
"Reflection, Summary, and Conclusion" chapter in, 152, 213n12
supernatural, the
the *do* list for moving naturally in, 49–50
the *don't* list for moving naturally in, 49
Supernatural Missions: The Impact of the Supernatural on World Missions (R. Clark), 45, 209n2 (chap. 7)

testimonies, 55–56, 87, 108
and bringing God glory, 52
Jesus' testimony, 107–8
live testimonies, 146, 172
in the Old Testament, 210–11n3
questions to ask people giving healing testimonies, 172
video testimonies, 146, 168, 171–72, 203
theodicy, 36
There Is More! The Secret to Experiencing God's Power to Change Your Life (R. Clark), 98, 209n2 (chap. 10), 109–10n11
Third Wave movement, 213n10
Thompson, Helen and Bill, 81–82
"Till All Our Struggles Cease" (Price), 162
tongues, 121
as primarily directed toward God, 122
Toronto Blessing, 22
Trine, Ralph Waldo, 78–79
Truxel, Luke, 164
"two kingdoms at war" worldview, 188–89

Vineyard movement
as the antithesis of the Word of Faith movement, 82
emphasis of on the gifting of God, 82

Vineyard team, teaching of at Clark's Baptist church, 21–22
Visitatio Infirmorum, "The Trial and Examination of the Soul," 39

Wagner, C. Peter, 213n10
Wagner Leadership Institute of Global Awakening, "Missions 101—Raising the Dead," 207n3
warfare worldview, 36
emphasis of on spiritual warfare, 37
Weatherhead, Leslie, 144
What's Wrong with Protestant Theology? Tradition vs. Biblical Emphasis (Ruthven), 208n5, 212n3 (chap. 17), 214n1 (chap. 22)
White, Todd, 122, 211n5
Wimber, John, 25–26, 50, 108–9, 109, 122, 152
Word of Faith movement, 76–84
"confession-possession" as a major theme of, 82
effect of its positive message, 80–81
emphasis of on people's faith, 82
influence of the Faith Cure movement on, 78
overreaction to the position of, 76–84, 88–89
validation of, 81–83
word studies, 147
words of knowledge, 22, 109, 115, 140–41, 141, 146, 148, 166, 207n2
Baptist understanding of, 117
Bartimaeus as an illustration of, 166
and laying a foundation, 111–14
the process of giving words of knowledge, 167–68
purpose of, 112
reception of, 110–11
as revelation from God, 117–18
Words of Knowledge (R. Clark), 212n6
worldview. *See* blueprint worldview; "two kingdoms at war" worldview; warfare worldview
Wounded Spirits (Weatherhead), 144

Dr. Randy Clark, overseer of Global Awakening and the Apostolic Network of Global Awakening, is best known for helping spark the move of God now affectionately labeled "the Toronto Blessing." In the years since, his influence has grown as an international speaker. Noted primarily for revival, healing and impartation, Randy's message is simple: "God wants to use you."

Randy has the unique ability to minister to many denominations and apostolic networks. These have included Roman Catholics, Messianic Jews, Methodists, many Pentecostal and charismatic congregations, and the largest Baptist churches in Argentina, Brazil and South Africa. He has also taken more than six thousand people with him on international ministry teams. His friend and co-author, Bill Johnson, says that the fastest way to increase in the supernatural is to accompany Randy on an international trip. Randy has traveled to fifty countries, and he continues to travel extensively to see that God's mandate on his life is fulfilled.

Randy received his M.Div. from The Southern Baptist Theological Seminary and his D.Min. from United Theological Seminary. He has authored or helped compile over forty books, as well as numerous training manuals and workbooks. In addition, he has published two curriculum sets regarding healing and has created master of divinity courses on physical healing at both United Theological Seminary and Regent University Divinity

School. He also has developed both the Christian Healing Certification Program (CHCP) and the Christian Prophetic Certification Program (CPCP) online, which have seen over 3,500 course enrollments during their first three years.

Randy and his wife, DeAnne, reside in Mechanicsburg, Pennsylvania. They have four adult children, all of whom are married, and five grandchildren. For more information about Randy Clark, his ministry and his resource materials, visit www .globalawakening.com. For information about his online courses, see www.healingcertification.com and www.propheticcertifi cation.com.

More from Randy Clark

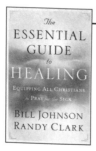

The ministry of healing is *not* reserved for a select few. In this practical, step-by-step guide, Bill Johnson and Randy Clark show how you, too, can become a powerful conduit of God's healing power.

The Essential Guide to Healing (with Bill Johnson)

For the first time, Bill Johnson and Randy Clark candidly share their personal journeys behind life in the healing spotlight. With honesty, humor and humility, they recount the failures, breakthroughs and time-tested advice that propelled them into effective ministry.

Healing Unplugged (with Bill Johnson)

Grace is more than receiving eternal life. God wants you to be a vessel of His glory. He wants to fill you with His Spirit and His gifts. He wants to give you *more*. With his trademark insight and encouragement, Randy Clark explains that *more* is not only biblical but essential for greater fruitfulness in ministry—and he shares how you can access *more* in your life today.

There Is More

 Chosen

Stay up-to-date on your favorite books and authors with our free e-newsletters. Sign up today at chosenbooks.com.

Find us on Facebook. facebook.com/chosenbooks

Follow us on Twitter. @Chosen_Books